P9-DIH-550

Can Globalization Succeed?

The Big Idea

Dena Freeman

Can Globalization Succeed?

A primer for the 21ˢᵗ century

Over 160 illustrations

General Editor:
Matthew Taylor

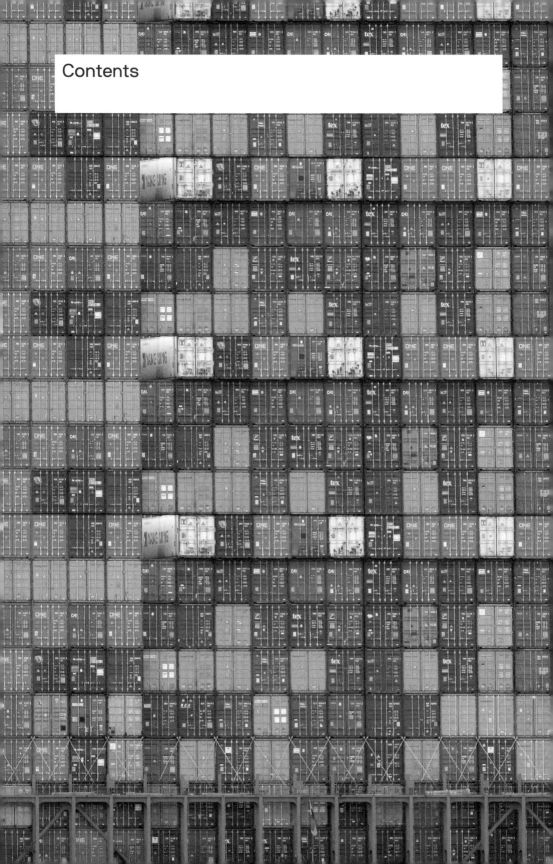

Contents

Introduction

A

Can globalization succeed? This
is the question on the lips of policy-
makers and ordinary people alike,
as the world appears to teeter on
the brink of fundamental change.

Will globalization continue, especially in the wake of the
COVID-19 pandemic, or are we about to enter a new period
of nationalism? Is globalization a good thing? And if so, good
for whom? How does globalization relate to economic inequality,
to pandemics and to climate change? What would it mean for
globalization to succeed? Would a successful globalization
be a simple continuation of contemporary processes until
it reached some kind of stable endpoint or would it require
a radical transformation in the nature of globalization itself?

These are big and vital questions.
Globalization affects the lives of
just about everyone on the planet
and thus questions about the future
of globalization are important for us all.

A Street art in Lisbon, Portugal, by artists Blu and Os Gêmeos, showing a businessman, crowned with the emblems of international oil companies, holding the earth in his hand and sucking it out with a straw.
B During the COVID-19 pandemic US President Donald Trump tried to foster nationalist and xenophobic sentiment by portraying the new virus as 'Chinese'.

In recent years, a number of scholars and commentators, such as Michael O'Sullivan, Stephen D. King, John Ralston Saul and Antimo Verde, have started to argue that globalization is over.

They point to the rise of populist politicians such as Donald Trump (b. 1946) and Viktor Orbán (b. 1963), who blame their respective country's problems on globalization and promise to build fences and tariff regimes to keep out foreign people and foreign goods, and more recently, 'foreign' viruses. These scholars claim that even before the COVID-19 pandemic, levels of world trade were beginning to decline, and they would see the precipitous fall in international trade, travel and tourism caused by responses to the pandemic as a further step in this direction. They argue that the world is heading towards a new phase of nationalism, racism and possibly even war.

B

Donald J. Trump ✔
@realDonaldTrump

I always treated the Chinese Virus very seriously, and have done a very good job from the beginning, including my very early decision to close the "borders" from China - against the wishes of almost all. Many lives were saved. The Fake News new narrative is disgraceful & false!

Others are not convinced. Scholars such as Michael Bordo and Moisés Naím find it hard to imagine that globalization is coming to an end and have instead argued that it is temporarily slowing down or 'resetting' after the 2008 financial crisis, and will most likely get back on course and continue to evolve in the coming years. More forcibly, Susan Lund and colleagues from the McKinsey Global Institute argue that despite the rise of nationalist rhetoric, at least before the COVID-19 pandemic, globalization was showing no signs of slowing down. They claim that rates of international trade and international capital mobility were at an all-time high. Furthermore, technological advances of the Internet and social media are increasingly connecting everyone in an ever-evolving social web. They maintain that despite the current blip, globalization is not only continuing, but even speeding up and deepening.

A third group of scholars and commentators, including David Held, Heikki Patomäki and Thomas Pogge, argue that the current form of globalization is inherently undemocratic and unjust, and that it is leading to increasing social, economic and health inequality all over the world. They claim that a different kind of globalization is needed, one that takes into account citizens' voices and shares the benefits more fairly.

A

In order to make sense of this diversity of opinions, and to understand what is going on in the world, it is necessary to first define more precisely what we mean by globalization. Broadly speaking, the term 'globalization' is used in different ways to mean three quite different things.

A   Guests at a 'Sakura Hanami' (cherry blossom viewing) party in Tokyo, Japan, mix local tradition with global food as they eat Kentucky Fried Chicken under the cherry blossom.

B   McDonald's has mixed global forms with local tastes as it has spread around the world. This family in Casablanca, Morocco, for example, may just have eaten the 'McArabia', a sandwich of grilled kofta wrapped in pitta bread.

Some people use the term to refer to a general interconnectedness of people around the world. They focus on the increasing flows of people, goods and ideas across borders. In this view, globalization is Italian people eating sushi and Japanese people eating hamburgers. Globalization is Indians watching Hollywood films and Africans watching Bollywood films. It is instantaneous communication with anyone, anywhere; it is tourism, travel and Facebook leading to an increasing exchange of tastes, ideas and culture.

B

A

Global governance is the attempt to manage global processes in the absence of a global government. It consists of a fragmented mix of international agreements, international organizations and informal arrangements between states, business and civil society.

A   People in a remote part of Mali take part in global culture by watching a World Cup football match on a television supplied by solar energy.
B   The United Nations Security Council is the most powerful body of the UN and plays a major role in contemporary global governance.
C   The Thai fishing industry, which supplies many global supermarkets, relies on the cheap labour of modern-day slaves, often trafficked from other countries and forced onto fishing boats where they are trapped against their will.

B

Other people use the term 'globalization' to mean a process in which human social systems expand from the national level to the global level, and that will eventually lead to a time when everyone on the planet is part of one shared society with a shared global political system, a shared global economic system, a shared global health system, and a shared global ecology. In this usage, globalization is far more than increasing cross-border interconnections between people. It is also quite different from the idea of 'internationalization', in which an 'international community' is composed of separate, cooperating or competing, nation states.

In this view globalization is advancing at different speeds in different areas. While the economy is already highly globalized, with national markets increasingly integrated into the global market, other areas are globalizing more slowly. Society and culture are beginning to globalize in certain domains, with for example, fully half of the world's population watching the football matches of the World Cup in 2018 and almost 60% being on the Internet, sharing films, music, news and ideas. The globalization of the political system is advancing more slowly, with the gradual increase in processes of 'global governance' and the development of largely powerless international organizations, such as the World Health Organization (WHO).

A third use of the term 'globalization' refers to a specific economic model that is often called neoliberal globalization. This posits the globalization of markets, the globalization of production and trade, and the globalization of companies in the form of transnational corporations (TNCs), while politics and regulation remain at the level of the nation state.

In this model the nature of the state transforms in order to meet the needs of freely flowing global capital. Instead of regulating the economy and taxing corporate profits to use for redistribution and the public good, states instead reduce taxes and regulations as they compete with other states to attract in-flows of global capital. Globalization in this sense is a global level economy but a national level politics. It is transnational corporations paying little tax, while everyone else finds their tax bills rising. It is falling labour standards, increasing pollution and rising greenhouse gas emissions, as global businesses find ways to escape government regulation.

C

It is this particular type of globalization that has come to dominate our lives. When people argue about whether or not globalization is over, they are talking about this kind of globalization. This book looks at how neoliberal globalization emerged in the 1980s and explores how its workings have differently affected rich countries and poor countries, and the rich and the poor within them. It considers whether this type of globalization is compatible with democracy and tracks the subtle process of de-democratization that has accompanied its rise.

In order to address the broader question of whether globalization can succeed, however, it is necessary to broaden out the definition of globalization into something closer to the second meaning. Asking 'Can globalization succeed?' is not the same as asking 'Can neoliberal globalization succeed?'

A

De-democratization refers to the regression or breakdown of democracy. It can include reductions in civil and political freedoms, the removal of economic or other matters from democratic control, and even the transition from a democratic to an authoritarian government.

B

C

A   US President Donald Trump campaigned on a strongly pro-nationalist and anti-globalization platform, promising to put 'America first'.
B   Poor people in India maintain social distance as they wait to receive rations during the COVID-19 pandemic.
C   India is the world's largest democracy, but the quality of its democracy is in decline. While voting is free and widespread, the Hindu nationalist agenda of Prime Minister Narendra Modi and his Bharatiya Janata party (BJP) has led to a harsh crackdown on political rights and civil liberties, particularly of Muslims, and the widespread suppression of dissent.

Indeed, for globalization to succeed it may be necessary to have a completely different form of globalization, one that takes into account citizens' concerns and that offers a mechanism for global coordination and collaboration necessary to tackle global problems, such as climate change, pandemics and economic inequality.

The first three chapters of this book analyse the history of globalization, the impacts of contemporary globalization, and the anti-globalization backlash. Chapter four then explores some alternative forms of globalization, considers how globalization can be reconciled with democracy, and discusses what kind of globalization can, and should, succeed.

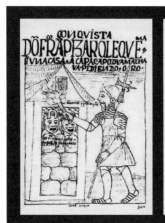

A

A An account of Peruvian history sent by a Peruvian noble to the King of Spain in 1615. In the 16th century Spanish conquistadors seized Mexico from the Aztec people and Peru from the Incas, plundered their riches and killed millions of native inhabitants.

B African slaves were subject to inhumane conditions on the slave ships, as shown in this picture by Isaac Robert Cruickshank from 1792.

C A slave auction in Richmond, Virginia, 1860. In the Americas, African slaves were bought and sold as commodities. In Africa, slave raiding led to the breakdown of local communities and the collapse of emergent state systems.

While complex systems of long-distance exchange first emerged thousands of years ago, and empires have waxed and waned across large swathes of Asia and Europe since *c.* 3000 BC, it was European sea-faring technology that eventually brought the whole world into one interconnected system.

At the end of the 14th century, the world consisted of large empires in Asia – most importantly the Ming dynasty (1368–1644) in China and the Mughal dynasty (1526–1857) in and around much of present-day India – and a range of small and medium-sized polities in Europe and Africa, all connected through various long-distance trade routes. Farther afield, other small and medium-sized polities existed in the Americas and in the Pacific, but as yet these areas were quite separate and unknown to each other. The development of Portuguese maritime expertise and the desire of the Portuguese king to take control of the lucrative spice trade between Asia and Europe ultimately led to the coming together of these separate spaces and the emergence of a truly global system. Since then, the interconnections have deepened and transformed as we move towards an increasingly globalized world.

The first wave of European colonialism started in the early 15th century, mainly led by Spain and Portugal. During the 15th and 16th centuries, the king of Portugal controlled much of the coast of Africa, major areas of southern India and South East Asia, and parts of what is now Brazil, while the king of Spain controlled most of what was known of the Americas. Whereas the Portuguese focused on trade, the Spanish decided to form large settlements in their colonies. Thousands of Spaniards flocked to the Americas to explore and settle the new lands.

The territory was, of course, not empty, but full of native peoples, and a series of violent wars ensued as the local people sought to defend themselves and their resources against the foreign invaders. Europeans also brought new diseases to the Americas, including smallpox, measles, typhus and cholera, leading to the deaths of millions of native people. On their return home, European sailors brought syphilis to Europe, which though less lethal caused great social disruption across the continent.

In their search for cheap labour to work on the plentiful American lands, the Spanish and Portuguese developed the transatlantic slave trade. In 1526, the Portuguese made the first transatlantic slave voyage, bringing slaves from Africa to Brazil, and over the next 300 years some 12 million Africans were abducted from their communities, sold to Europeans and brought to the Americas as slaves to work in appalling conditions in the plantations and mines.

B

C

As voyagers travelled back and forth between Europe, Africa and the Americas, they brought with them animals, plants, fungi, diseases, technologies, minerals and ideas, changing lives and landscapes on both sides of the ocean. Known as the 'Columbian exchange', this movement of goods between the New World and the Old World can be thought of as the first globalization – the globalization of crops and diseases.

In **mercantile capitalism**, or mercantilism, money is made mainly by buying goods from a market where they are cheap and then transporting them and selling them in a market where they are expensive.

Chartered trading companies included the Dutch East India Company, the Royal African Company and the Hudson's Bay Company. The first major chartered trading company was the Muscovy Company, formed in 1555 and given a monopoly to trade between England and Muscovy (a principality centred around Moscow).

In the **Industrial Revolution** (1760–1840) new manufacturing processes were developed which made use of machines, steam engines and chemical agents, leading to the rise of the mechanized factory system.

A second wave of European colonialism took place in the 17th and 18th centuries as France, Britain and the Netherlands began to compete with Spain and Portugal for control of territories around the world. During this period, the form of colonialism also began to change, linked to the emergence of an early form of capitalism known as mercantile capitalism. Instead of being carried out by individuals on behalf of the king, colonial activities were increasingly carried out by chartered trading companies: joint-stock companies that had received a monopoly over a particular trade from the king. In essence, these chartered companies were the first transnational corporations (TNCs). However, in contrast to today's corporations, which are seen as part of the private sector and quite distinct from the state, these chartered companies were in some senses arms of the emerging state.

A   An 18th-century portrayal of a British East India Company official riding on an elephant. At the height of its power the company ruled over one-fifth of the world's people, ran a huge private army and generated a revenue greater than that of the whole of Britain.

Their charters gave them not only a monopoly over a particular trade, but also sovereign powers over the lands where they traded. They could wage wars, set up forts and trading posts, print money, impose duties and tariffs, enter into treaties, administer justice and generally rule the local population. Wars could be waged between rival corporations abroad without the European states getting involved.

During the 19th century, a number of political, economic and technological changes took place in Europe, which brought about the modern world order and set the scene for real economic globalization. States became the basic unit of political organization, the Industrial Revolution set in motion a global system of production, exchange and consumption, and workers and poor people began to demand democracy and political emancipation.

A

A An illustration of the battle between British soldiers and citizens of Boston in 1770 that became known as the 'Boston Massacre'. In the late 18th century the thirteen colonies fought against the British and eventually gained independence in 1776. Similar wars of independence soon followed in Latin America and by 1830 almost all of the Americas, with the exception of Canada, had gained independence and become sovereign states in their own right.

B A fire in Josefplatz, Vienna, Austria, during the 1848 revolution. A wave of revolutions known as the 'People's Spring' or the 'Spring of Nations' erupted in over 50 European countries in 1848 as people sought to remove old imperial and monarchical structures and replace them with independent, democratic nation-states.

C Karl Marx depicted holding his analysis of capitalist society, *Das Kapital* (1867), and pointing to a bright socialist future. Marx inspired workers to agitate and rise up in order to build a more just social order in which everyone together would own the means of production.

Sovereign states are political entities that have one centralized government that has sovereignty over a specific territory. They came into being in Europe during the 17th and 18th centuries. Before that, in the medieval period, there was a mix of city states, fiefdoms, kingdoms and empires. None of these were sovereign, because the Pope and the Catholic Church could intervene in their affairs.

By the end of the 18th century, sovereign states had emerged as the main unit in which society and politics were organized in Europe and the Americas. While European overseas empire would continue for another 150 years, and indeed expand, the course had now been set towards the world of independent sovereign states, which would finally come fully into being in the late 20th century.

During the same period, the scientific revolution and Enlightenment, with their focus on reason, progress and liberty, had brought forward new theories of government. The philosophy of liberalism, with its idea that all people should be considered as citizens of the state, with equal rights and equal representation, had begun to catch the public imagination. In 1789 the French Revolution sought to sweep away the traditional, hierarchically structured 'ancien régime' and to establish instead a democratic republic based on Enlightenment ideals of liberty, equality and democracy.

Over the course of the 19th century, a long process of democratization took place in Europe.

At the start of the century, the right to vote in most European countries was restricted only to wealthy male landowners, who accounted on average for about 2% of the population. The other 98% had no representation in parliament and thus no political voice. The new industrial entrepreneurs and the factory workers alike found this unacceptable. A wave of protest movements sprang up across Europe, including, for example, the Chartist movement in the UK, as ordinary working-class people demanded the right to political representation. In some countries, there were strikes, protests and demonstrations; in other countries there were revolutions. All in all, it took around 100 years of major political struggle before the landed elites finally gave up their monopoly on the vote and brought in a system of universal male suffrage.

The **Chartists** were a working-class movement in the UK calling for the right to vote for all men. In 1838 they drew up a People's Charter demanding a range of reforms, including universal male suffrage, voting by secret ballot and parliamentary elections every year. They presented petitions with millions of signatures to the House of Commons and carried out mass demonstrations.

B

C

A   The suffragettes fought for women's right to vote using civil disobedience, including chaining themselves to railings, setting fire to postboxes and getting arrested. Emmeline Pankhurst (right) was arrested seven times before women's suffrage was approved.

B   As this cartoon from 1904 shows, there was strong public feeling against huge corporations. Standard Oil is portrayed here as an octopus with tentacles wrapped around the steel, copper and shipping industries, and with another tentacle reaching for the White House.

Free trade philosophy claimed that markets would flourish better without the involvement of the state. It suggested that the state should limit its activities to national defence, the protection of property rights and the administration of justice, while the economy should be left to balance itself out according to the 'hidden hand of the market'.

Adam Smith (1723–90) was a Scottish economist. He is considered by many to be the 'Father of Capitalism'.

Even when all men had been given the vote, a further struggle ensued to extend the vote to women. By the early to mid 20th century, democracy had been achieved in most European countries and most citizens finally had the right to vote. As we shall see, this would greatly change the dynamics of the economic globalization that was beginning to unfold.

Alongside these developments, a new economic philosophy began to prevail. Instead of mercantilism, politicians and businessmen began to embrace the philosophy of free trade, first promoted by Adam Smith in his book *The Wealth of Nations* (1776) and eventually becoming mainstream in the second part of the 19th century.

Smith argued that states should not protect local businesses from foreign competitors with trade tariffs and import quotas, but should let them compete on the open market. He also maintained that states should not allocate monopolies to companies, and that companies should not carry out political activities for the state. Instead, he insisted that there should be separate public and private sectors.

As a result of this thinking, during the 19th century corporations became more independent of government control and evolved into something closer to the corporations we know today. European states started to rule the colonies directly, and the corporations stopped carrying out official state activities and began to focus more specifically on just making profit. Through a process of mergers and acquisitions, they grew massively in size until, by the latter part of the century, there was a relatively small number of huge corporations that controlled most of the major infrastructure industries, such as oil, steel, railroads and shipping. However, many of these large corporations used shady practices to dominate markets and increase their wealth: forming cartels to fix prices, taking payment from other corporations in order to not compete with them, driving out smaller companies in order to form monopolies, and employing lobbyists to influence government. As a result, many of the US businessmen behind the largest corporations, such as John Rockefeller (1839–1937) and Andrew Carnegie (1835–1919), came to be known as 'robber barons'.

B

THE "DAILY MAIL" COMMERCIAL MAP OF AFRICA.

THE CAPE-TOWN TO CAIRO ROUTE.

A

A   This 19th-century map of Africa shows how European colonial powers divided up the continent. France got most of West Africa, Britain got much of East and Southern Africa, and most of the rest was split between Germany, Belgium and Portugal. Only Ethiopia and Liberia remained independent.

B   Illustrations of 19th-century cloth dying and trading in India. The vibrant Indian textile industry declined under colonialism because the British placed high tariffs on Indian cloth while keeping British cloth tariff free.

In **industrial capitalism**, money is made mainly by producing large volumes of goods using industrial machinery and the labour of workers. Capitalists are able to accumulate wealth because they own the means of production.

The Industrial Revolution and the shift from mercantile capitalism to industrial capitalism caused the world economy to transition towards a globalized system of production centred around European states. European factories required a steady supply of raw materials, such as oil, rubber and manganese, industrialists sought to expand their markets globally in order to sell more products, and businessmen and bankers with excess capital wanted to invest overseas.

The colonies thus took on a new importance and the 19th century witnessed a third wave of colonialism as more territories were colonized, particularly in the Far East and in Africa. Technological improvements, such as the railway, steamship and telegraph, allowed faster and cheaper transport and communications, and thus enabled businesses to begin to operate on a truly global scale.

In this newly emerging system of global industrial capitalism, the global economy began to have a centre and a periphery. The European countries were at the centre, with a strong manufacturing industry, whereas the colonies were at the periphery, supplying raw materials for European factories and then providing a market for the final products. Colonies that tried to industrialize found that European trade policy made it impossible. Despite the free trade philosophy, the Europeans placed high import tariffs on manufactured goods from the colonies and yet allowed no import duties on European manufactured goods sold to the colonies. This ensured that manufactured goods from the colonies could not compete with those from the European countries.

The world began to diverge into rich countries and poor countries.

B

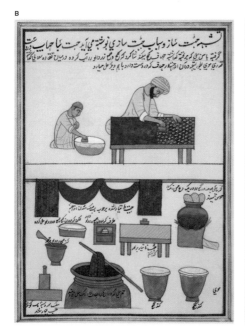

By 1870, everything was in place for the first era of economic globalization – an interlinked system of sovereign states (with overseas empires) and a global economy in which capital and goods could flow across borders fairly freely. The period between 1870 and 1914 is often referred to as the 'Belle Époque' or the 'first globalization'. There were high levels of international trade, cross-border capital flows and labour migration as the economy took on a truly global form. Taken altogether, the levels were similar to those today. The economist John Maynard Keynes (1883–1946) famously described life in these years: 'The inhabitant of London could order by telephone, sipping his morning tea in bed, the various products of the whole Earth, in such quantity as he might see fit, and reasonably expect their early delivery upon his doorstep.'

However, trying to create a system of national economies and national societies within a global sea of capital led to some difficult problems and trade-offs.

A

The **exchange rate** is the price of one currency in terms of another currency at a particular point in time. Exchange rates can be either fixed or floating. Fixed exchange rates are decided by a country's central bank, whereas floating exchange rates are decided by the mechanism of market demand and supply.

The **gold standard** was a system in which international trade was backed by gold and the values of different currencies were fixed according to an equivalent amount of gold. For example, the British pound sterling was defined as 113 grains of pure gold and the US dollar as 23.22 grains. So, one British pound equalled 113/23.22 or 4.87 US dollars.

B

C

A   The first period of globalization was a time of huge migration. More than 160 million people, such as this Indian family in German East Africa (above) and this Dutch family arriving in New York, USA (below), moved around the world in search of better opportunities.

B   Workers in the smelting room of the US mint in Philadelphia, c. 1900.

C   Gold bars being weighed on huge scales at the US Mint.

During this period, European governments allowed the free flow of capital in and out of their countries and also implemented a system of fixed exchange rates in order to facilitate international trade and keep the global financial system stable.

Exchange rates were fixed according to the gold standard. This system facilitated trade between buyers and sellers from countries with different currencies, and also maintained a balance between the different countries. If a country imported more than it exported, then there would be a net out-flow of gold from that country's central bank. Since money had to be backed by gold, this would result in a reduction in the money supply in that country, which in turn would lead to a fall in prices of locally produced goods. These goods would then become more competitive on the global market and the amount of exports would increase. This would result in a net in-flow of gold back into the country. This process, known as the 'price-specie flow mechanism', stopped countries racking up large trade surpluses or trade deficits and kept prices aligned in different countries.

However, in this system, governments found that they could not keep control of national monetary policy. They could not print more money in order to stimulate local production or to increase levels of employment, for example, because the domestic money supply was determined solely by the amount of gold sitting in the central bank.

Thus, governments found that with economic globalization (capital mobility across borders) and a system of fixed exchange rates, they had little way to manage the national economy to ensure that it worked for the benefit of everyone.

This is an example of what later came to be known as the 'open economy trilemma'. In the 1960s economists John Marcus Fleming (1911–76) and Robert Mundell (b. 1932) independently realized that in an open economy, in which capital can freely move in and out across national borders, it is impossible for the national government to both keep control of monetary policy and to fix exchange rates. If they fix the exchange rate, then they lose control of monetary policy. And if they keep control of monetary policy, by changing interest rates in order to enlarge or reduce the money supply, then the value of their currency will change relative to the currencies of other countries, and thus there will have to be a system of floating exchange rates. The only way that the government can both fix exchange rates and keep control of monetary policy is if they insulate their currency from the global economy by restricting cross-border capital flows.

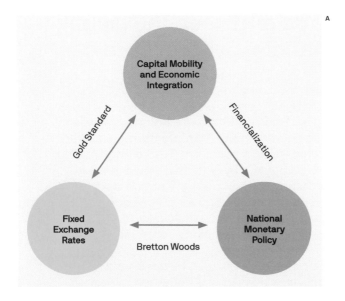

A

A   The Mundell-Fleming open economy trilemma. States can only ever have two out of three of the economic policies shown in the circles. The terms above the arrows show the resulting global economic system for each choice.

B   Dani Rodrik's open polity trilemma. States can only ever have two out of three of the political options shown in the circles. The terms above the arrows show the resulting global political system for each choice.

In other words, governments can only ever have two out of the following three macroeconomic measures: fixed exchange rates, independent national monetary policy and capital mobility.

Monetary policy is the policy that controls the supply of money in an economy. By altering interest rates, governments can, in effect, either print more money or take money out of the system. Changing the amount of money in the system can influence growth, inflation and employment.

Capital mobility refers to the ease of the process of moving financial capital between countries, for example, in bank transfers or when investing in a foreign country. Because large cross-border capital flows can severely disrupt a country's economy, governments sometimes impose capital controls which restrict the amount of money that is allowed to flow in or out of their country.

In the early 2000s economist Dani Rodrik suggested a related trilemma, which we can call the 'open polity trilemma'. This shows that it is only ever possible to have two out of the following three: sovereign states, democracy and capital mobility. A sovereign state with borders open to capital flows will have to implement policies that will attract capital and make that state competitive in the global market. It will therefore have to give up on democracy, because voters are unlikely to vote for policies that would cause them economic hardship. In order to have open capital flows and democracy, it would be necessary to move democratic politics up to the global level in which case sovereign states would cease to be important. The only way to have both sovereign states and democracy is to insulate the democratic state from the global economy by restricting cross-border capital flows.

B

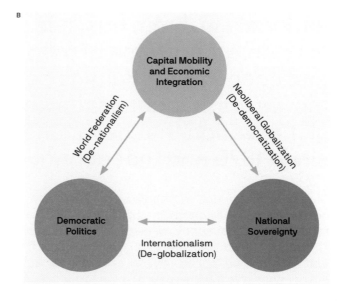

Capital Mobility and Economic Integration

World Federation (De-nationalism)

Neoliberal Globalization (De-democratization)

Democratic Politics

National Sovereignty

Internationalism (De-globalization)

A

Western governments have made different decisions with regard to these trilemmas, and this has largely determined whether they have favoured economic globalization or economic nationalism. From this, it is possible to understand some of the political and economic dynamics behind the waves of globalization and de-globalization that have taken place since 1870 and that continue today.

During the first period of globalization (1870–1914), governments chose capital mobility and fixed exchange rates and thus lost control of national monetary policy. This mainly served the interests of international traders and investors, by facilitating cross-border transactions, but did not serve the interests of local farmers and workers.

Cash-poor and debt-burdened farmers suffered greatly during periods of trade deficit when gold standard rules led to both falling prices and an increase in interest rates, and the urban proletariat suffered tremendously due to the high rates of unemployment that accompanied the gold standard system.

The **flu pandemic** of 1918–19 caused major social and economic disruption as governments imposed social-distancing measures, such as closing schools and churches and restricting public transport, while businesses slowed due to the high number of staff absences and deaths. As a result of the pandemic, many countries, including Canada, France, Australia, India, Iran and Russia, established or massively expanded their public health services.

Economic inequality within European countries grew rapidly. However, during this period, most farmers and factory workers did not yet have a vote in their national political systems, and thus the elites did not worry too much about their suffering. With capital mobility and sovereign states, but without democracy, the first period of globalization lasted for around 40 years.

In 1914 the system finally collapsed as rising tensions between the European states led to the First World War. Some 20 million people died in the war between 1914 and 1918, and a further 50 to 100 million died in the severe flu pandemic that spread around the world in 1918 and 1919. During the war, all governments suspended gold convertibility so that they could print more money in order to pay for the war effort, and they imposed tight capital controls to stop capital from leaving their countries.

A   This painting by Belgian artist Charles Hermans, 1875, shows wealthy revellers leaving a restaurant in the early hours, while a group of poor labourers walk past on their way to work. The first period of globalization was a time of extreme inequality.

B   This political cartoon from 1883 depicts the inequality of the time. Wealthy industrialists Cyrus Field, Jay Gould, Cornelius Vanderbilt and Russell Sage are shown with bellies full of dollars, sitting on a large raft being carried on the backs of low wage workers.

B

In 1919 representatives of some thirty states assembled at the Paris Peace Conference in order to establish the terms of the peace after the First World War. One of the main outcomes of this conference was the formation of the League of Nations, the first intergovernmental organization with the aim of preventing wars and settling international disputes through negotiation and arbitration. Previously, European leaders had come together to discuss important matters and sign treaties at ad hoc conferences held in different cities at different times. Now, after the ravages of the war, they decided to create a permanent institution to facilitate future discussion and cooperation.

Once calm and normality returned, leaders began to think about how to put globalization back together again. During the 1920s, while the health section of the League of Nations considered how states could work together and share information to control the transmission of infectious diseases, the economic section tried to help governments coordinate a return to the gold standard so that international trade and finance could resume and the global economy could stabilize.

A

The **League of Nations** was based in Geneva, Switzerland, and was organized according to the tripartite division of powers in a parliamentary democracy – with an executive council (like a government), an assembly (like a parliament) and a secretariat (like a civil service). In many ways, it looked like a kind of world government, but in reality it had virtually no power to enforce its decisions.

Keynesian economics, named after British economist John Maynard Keynes, focused more on issues of demand, in contrast to classical liberal economics, which focused more on supply.

A   Vintage postcard from Ukraine c. 1917, featuring Russian revolutionary Vladimir Lenin and proclaiming 'Immortal Glory to the Proletarian Revolution'.

B   Discussions at the Paris Peace Conference took place during the 1919 flu pandemic. Georges Clemenceau (France), Woodrow Wilson (US) and Lloyd George (UK), pictured leaving the Palace of Versailles after signing the Treaty of Versailles on 28 June 1919, had all been ill with the flu.

By this time, democracy had been implemented in most European states, giving workers and farmers political representation and the right to vote. So, when the gold standard policies started again to lead to low wages and high unemployment, workers began to get involved with new political parties that represented their interests.

Just a few years earlier, in 1917, disgruntled workers had overthrown the Tsar in the Russian Revolution, and at this time Lenin (1870–1924) and the Bolsheviks were in the process of setting up a system of communist rule in Russia. European governments realized that if they continued to ignore workers' concerns, then a workers' party might be voted into power. Thus, in 1931, Britain left the gold standard and started to use national monetary policy to increase the money supply and reduce unemployment. Other countries quickly followed suit, and by the mid-1930s the gold standard was dead. After the New York stock market crash of 1929, many countries instigated capital controls to limit capital flight and imposed high trade barriers and tariffs.

The first era of globalization was now well and truly over.

The theory of free trade lay in tatters. Instead new economic theories arose, which argued that the government needed to protect the local economy against international trade and capital flows. Keynesian economics became the new mainstream and governments started to intervene in the economy for domestic purposes: expanding the money supply in order to reduce unemployment, increasing redistribution so that local workers would have enough money to buy goods and broadening welfare provisions for those who remained out of work.

"WIR NEHMEN DAS SCHICKSAL DER NATION IN DIE HÄNDE!"

Hitler wird Reichspräsident

A

The **United Nations (UN)** is an intergovernmental organization with the aim of maintaining world peace and security. Its headquarters are in New York, USA, while its many specialized agencies are located in major cities around the world. It is the most representative of all international organizations and its membership has expanded from 51 member states at its founding to 193 member states today.

In Germany, the economic crisis of the 1930s was particularly severe and when US banks withdrew their loans after the stock market crash, the resulting chaos left almost 30% of the population unemployed. In this extreme situation, politics became increasingly polarized with people turning to populist leaders on both the left and the right of the political spectrum. In 1933, Adolph Hitler's (1889–1945) Nazi party came to power, promising to increase trade barriers, promote national economic self-sufficiency and provide jobs. His racist, xenophobic and authoritarian policies soon led him to pull out of the League of Nations and to take the country to war. Between 1939 and 1945, Europe thus found itself again bathed in the blood of a world war.

It was clear that the League of Nations had not succeeded in preventing war and that a different kind of international organization was required. After the Second World War, many different options were discussed, ranging from a loose talking shop to a democratic world federation. In the end, leaders could only agree to an organization very similar to the League of Nations but with marginally more powers to intervene in certain situations of war. In 1945, the United Nations (UN) was founded, with a General Assembly open to all sovereign states but with no ability to enforce decisions, a small Security Council with some very limited real power, and several technical agencies, such as the World Health Organization (WHO) and the Food and Agriculture Organization (FAO).

The leading powers also met to discuss how to manage the global economy in a world in which domestic politics had become of great importance. They came together at Bretton Woods, USA, in 1944 and developed a system that restricted international capital flows and thus allowed governments to both fix their exchange rates and keep control of their own monetary policy. Currency exchange rates were fixed according to a kind of revised gold standard, in which all currencies were valued in relation to the US dollar, and the dollar was convertible to gold at the fixed rate of $35 per ounce. This system allowed national economies to protect themselves against global capital, while at the same time encouraging international trade in goods and commodities.

A   A Nazi propaganda poster from during Hitler's campaign to be Reich President, 1930s. The text states: 'We will take the fate of the nation into our hands!'
B   The Dutch delegation having informal discussions on the terrace during the Bretton Woods conference.
C   Formal negotiations at the Bretton Woods conference. Delegates came from 44 countries and worked for 22 days in three commissions: one dealing with the IMF, chaired by Harry Dexter White; one dealing with the World Bank, chaired by John Maynard Keynes; and one dealing with other means of financial cooperation, chaired by Mexican Finance Minister, Eduardo Suárez.

A

Two new international organizations
were set up: the International Monetary
Fund (IMF) and the World Bank. The remit
of the IMF was to maintain the stability
of the international financial system
and in particular to manage the regime
of fixed exchange rates and to provide
short-term loans to countries with
balance of payment difficulties. The
main task of the World Bank, initially,
was to provide loans for post-war
reconstruction in Europe.

There were also discussions about how to organize international
trade, but these were far more contentious. The US negotiating
team, led by Harry Dexter White (1892–1948), proposed a system
of unregulated free trade. But other countries, which were mostly
in debt to the USA, feared that this would lead to the strongest
countries amassing huge trade surpluses and incredible
power, while other countries would spiral in a downward cycle
because their debts would lead them to run up trade deficits,
which in turn would force them to take on more debt.

B

A Opening session of the Second Annual Meetings of the Boards of Governors of the World Bank and International Monetary Fund at the Institute of Civil Engineers in London, 11 September 1947.

B Belgian foreign minister, Paul van Zeeland, signs the Treaty of Paris in 1951, establishing the European Coal and Steel Community, with the aim to integrate the coal and steel industries of France, Western Germany, Belgium, the Netherlands, Luxembourg and Italy, so that further war in Europe would be impossible, and to lay the groundwork for the later creation of the European Union.

The British negotiating team, led by Keynes and with widespread support from European and Latin American countries, proposed a system that would balance trade more fairly. They proposed the establishment of an international clearing union with its own currency – the bancor – which would be exchangeable with other currencies at a fixed rate of exchange. A range of mechanisms would incentivize countries to end the year with zero bancors, such that they had neither a trade surplus nor a trade deficit. The system would stop countries with a trade surplus from becoming too powerful, and would also prevent countries with a trade deficit from spiralling into larger deficits and more debt.

White, however, refused. He argued for what was best for the US national interest, not what would have been best for the world system as a whole. He told Keynes and the British parliament that if they did not accept his proposal they would not receive their next war loan. White's system was duly instigated.

In the following years, many countries found themselves stuck in a debt crisis, as Keynes had predicted. It is thus not surprising that in recent years the idea of an international clearing union and a shared reserve currency to balance international trade has re-emerged in several places.

In the early 2000s, a group of Latin American countries instituted such a system within the ALBA regional trading bloc, with a regional clearing union and a regional currency, called the sucre (see Chapter 4). And at the G20 meeting in 2009, the governor of the People's Bank of China, Zhou Xiaochuan (b. 1948), suggested that Keynes's proposal had perhaps been better than White's and that the world needed a uniform global reserve currency to stabilize and balance the economy.

A

ALBA was founded in 2004. At its peak, its members included Venezuela, Cuba, Bolivia, Nicaragua, Dominica, Ecuador and the small Caribbean states of St Vincent and the Grenadines, Antigua and Barbuda, St Lucia, Grenada, and St Kitts and Nevis.

B

The **G20**, or Group of 20, was formed in 1999 as a forum for finance ministers from 19 countries plus the EU to coordinate global financial stability. After the financial crash of 2008 the G20 was upgraded to become a forum for country leaders and their meetings were institutionalized in an annual summit.

A The leader of the Indonesian National Party, Sukarno (1902–70), addresses a rally demanding independence from the Netherlands. Sukarno went on to become Indonesia's first president in 1945.

B A parade of the Quit India Movement, calling for the end of British rule. India gained independence in 1947 and Jawaharlal Nehru (1889–1964) became its first prime minister.

C Tanzanian prime minister designate Julius Nyerere (1922–99) is carried on supporters' shoulders from the State House in Dar es Salaam during celebrations in 1961 to mark the country's forthcoming independence.

C

The Bretton Woods system worked reasonably well for around 30 years.

During this period of internationalism, the industrial countries recovered from the war and became prosperous. Since capital flows were restricted, it was possible to have both sovereign states and democracy. As a result of mass democratic politics, most European countries set up wide-ranging welfare states, with taxation enabling governments to provide education, health care and social services. This was a time of high social mobility as the children of coal miners and factory workers could attain a good education, access decent health care, and get a well-paying job that secured them a higher standard of living than previous generations.

During the 1950s and early 1960s, European countries finally relinquished most of their colonies and more than 100 new independent countries came into being, primarily in Africa and Asia. These new countries, often referred to as 'developing countries', started the complex task of trying to meld their diverse populations into a 'nation' and transforming their economy from one of colonial dependence to one of an independent sovereign state. During the 1960s, many of the first leaders of these states implemented socialist policies and most of them experienced solid levels of economic growth.

A

B

A A protest against
unemployment
and inflation in
Chicago, 1973.
B Workers striking for
a pay rise at a steel
plant in Duisburg,
Germany, 1973.
The sign says 'This
company is on strike.'
C US President Ronald
Reagan and British
Prime Minister
Margaret Thatcher,
seen here dancing
together at the
White House in 1988,
were the political
initiators of neoliberal
globalization.
D Commodity traders
at the London Oil and
Petroleum Futures
Exchange in 1983.

However, in the early 1970s, the system began to break down. During the 1960s, the USA printed a lot of money to pay for rising imports and for the Vietnam War (1955–75). This led to high inflation and more dollars in the global economy than could be backed by gold. The only way to balance the system would have been for the USA to stop printing money and to instigate unpopular austerity measures. As the most powerful country, the USA could not be forced to do this, and instead it continued to print money. Other countries with high dollar reserves began to get nervous and some of them started to bring their dollars to the US Federal Reserve for conversion to gold. Seeing what was happening, the USA closed the gold window at the Federal Reserve and announced that it would no longer convert dollars to gold. It, thus, unilaterally ended the Bretton Woods era and caused the world to move to a system of free-floating exchange rates.

Around the same time, corporations were beginning to feel the impacts of the post-war national settlements with labour. Strong trade unions, relatively high wages and the political entitlements of the welfare states were impinging on their profits.

C

D

As new technologies, such as improvements to commercial aeroplanes and container ships, and early versions of fibre optics and mobile phones, were leading to reductions in transport and communication costs, corporations began to push to break out of the national restrictions. They lobbied for the removal of capital controls so that they could invest and do business beyond the national context.

In the 1980s, the USA removed all its capital controls and deregulated its financial industry. Other industrialized countries quickly followed suit. The era of internationalism was over and the world entered a second period of globalization. Capital could again flow increasingly freely across borders. This time, in contrast to the first period of globalization, governments kept control of monetary policy and allowed exchange rates to float.

In the following years, there was a massive increase in foreign direct investment as corporations set up new factories overseas or bought up foreign companies so that they became huge transnational corporations (TNCs). Between 1970 and 2008 the number of TNCs grew from about 7,000 to more than 77,000. There was also a rapid growth in international finance and the globalization of financial markets. The lack of global regulation, though, meant that the whole system became extremely unstable and prone to financial crashes.

During the 1980s, intense pressure was exerted on the developing countries to open their borders and integrate into the new globalizing economy.

The IMF and the World Bank used their leverage to persuade developing countries to liberalize their economies and open themselves to global trade and capital flows, whether they liked it or not. They did this by adding policy conditions to their loans, such that if a country needed a loan it would have to implement a range of 'structural adjustments' to its economy:

A

B

open up its markets to foreign competition, privatize many state-owned enterprises, promote private sector development, reduce corporate taxation and business regulation, devalue the currency and implement austerity policies to reduce public spending. Since most developing countries were desperate for loans during the 1980s and 1990s, the IMF and World Bank were able to effectively force them to open their borders and enter the global economy.

A   A palm oil plantation in Sabah, Malaysia. In the 1980s the IMF pushed Malaysia to increase its production of palm oil, leading to the country becoming one of the world's largest producers. Palm oil is widely used in processed foods, beauty products and in biofuels.

B   US President George H. W. Bush and Soviet leader Mikhail Gorbachev shake hands at the end the US-Soviet Summit in July 1991, just months before the dissolution of the USSR.

In 1989, the Berlin Wall came down. Soon afterwards, the Soviet Union collapsed and the Cold War came to an end. Russia and the other post-Soviet states ceased to espouse communism and instead embraced capitalism and entered the global economy. With both the developing countries and the Soviet bloc joining the globalizing capitalist system, political scientist Francis Fukuyama famously declared 'the end of history'. By this, he meant that there were no longer any ideological challenges to capitalism and liberal democracy. It seemed as if all the countries in the world would now adopt the same approach – sovereign states with liberal democracies and consumerist cultures, competing in the global free market.

A

A   A technician tests a wireless headset in preparation for the opening ceremony of the first WTO Ministerial Conference, Singapore, 1996.

B   Food banks, like this one in California, are charities that offer food to people who cannot afford to buy enough themselves. They have been common in the US since the 1980s, and started in Europe after the 2008 financial crisis.

During the 1990s, globalization went into over-drive, as rates of cross-border trade and capital flows increased rapidly, fuelled by new Internet technologies. In 1995, the World Trade Organization (WTO) was formed to further coordinate the removal of trade barriers between countries. A range of other international or transnational organizations were also set up and politicians and academics began to talk about 'global governance'. This implied that the global economic system was being governed, even though there was no global government.

The dominant economic theory was now neoliberalism, a refined version of 19th-century liberalism, with its emphasis on free trade, low regulation, low taxation and low public spending.

Neoliberal ideology called for states to reverse the policies that they had implemented during the Bretton Woods era, when they had set up welfare states to drive national equality and balance national economies. It recommended instead that they reduce government spending on redistribution and on welfare, cut public services and leave everything, or as much as possible, to the logic of the global market.

But how could this be achieved when states were democratic? Surely the population would not agree to this change of policy, which so clearly went against their interests?

B

2. The Impact of Globalization Today

A

Contemporary globalization has many similarities to the first era of globalization in the late 19th century, but also several important differences.

First, contemporary globalization is taking place in a context in which European empires no longer exist and the entire world is organized into separate sovereign states. Second, contemporary globalization is occurring in a context where democratic national politics has become the expected norm. Third, whereas in the first period of globalization policy-makers chose to have capital mobility and fixed exchange rates (thus losing control of national monetary policy), in contemporary globalization, policy-makers have chosen to combine capital mobility with monetary policy, and have thus initiated a system of floating exchange rates.

And fourth, new technologies, such as computers and the Internet, have enabled a much closer integration of social, political and economic systems.

Contemporary globalization can be characterized by a renewed and more integrated globalized system of production and exchange, a new system of globalized culture and consumption, and a radically transformed and expanded global financial sector. As the open polity trilemma predicted, these changes have been accompanied by a process of de-democratization. This chapter looks at these dynamics, and their consequences, in more detail.

A A busy street scene in São Paulo, Brazil's most populous city. Since the 1980s globalization has caused a rapid increase in urbanization the world over. Now more than 50% of the world's population live in cities.

B A passer-by checks the electronic stock market reader board in downtown Tokyo. Japan's financial markets were deregulated and internationalized in the 1980s and for a short time the Tokyo Stock Exchange was one of the largest securities markets in the world.

C A currency trader watches monitors at the foreign exchange dealing room of the KEB Hana Bank in Seoul, South Korea. Following large injections of foreign investment in the 1980s, Asian financial markets grew rapidly in the 1990s.

A

B

A   In the garment sector manufacturing was first outsourced to countries such as China, Singapore and Hong Kong in the 1980s, then moved to Indonesia, Thailand, Mexico and Turkey when they could offer cheaper labour, and has more recently shifted again to places such as Bangladesh (pictured here), Vietnam and Ethiopia.

B   Workers at a packhouse in Kenya prepare green beans for export to the EU and UK. Kenya started growing green beans in the late 1970s and exports grew rapidly in the 1980s and 1990s.

C   Known as the 'elephant chart' because it resembles an elephant with a raised trunk, this graph, based on the work of economist Branko Milanović, shows that the gains from globalization have been very unevenly distributed.

The removal of capital controls in the 1980s led to a massive increase in foreign direct investment into a number of emerging economies, particularly in China, India and across Asia, and the rise of a highly integrated system of globalized production. Wages are generally very low in these countries, sometimes as low as $2 or $3 per day, and regulatory standards are even lower. This makes the cost of production far cheaper than in more developed countries. The result has been a major shift in the distribution of world industry, as companies have moved low-skilled production from developed to developing countries and from well-regulated factories to sweatshops.

This has led to massive urbanization in these emerging countries, with the associated problems of overcrowding, poor sanitation and increasing environmental pollution, alongside the growth of a new middle class and a new urban poor. In the developed countries, it has led to a major loss of low-skilled manufacturing jobs and rising unemployment. The factories that remain in the developed countries have to cut costs to try to compete with those in the developing countries, and this leads to falling wages and an increase in part-time and casual work for the jobs that still exist.

As countries find themselves competing to attract global capital, a race to the bottom in standards and incentives has taken place.

Labour standards, health and safety standards and environmental standards have steadily fallen across much of the world. Governments compete with each other as to who can offer the lowest paid workers with the least protections. Trade unions have been restricted or banned in many countries and labour's ability to organize and to demand improvements has been massively reduced. Pollution levels and carbon emissions have soared.

Along with the globalization of industrial production, there has also been a globalization of agri-business and food production. Small-scale farmers have increasingly been pushed off their land or forced to work as outgrowers for large industrialized plantations. Large swathes of land have been put under monoculture production, leading to a reduction in both biodiversity and soil fertility. Large corporations are pushing the use of new seed varieties and genetically modified organisms (GMOs). Forests have been cut down to make more land available for agriculture and livestock production, leading to a reduction in their role in carbon sequestration and contributing to climate change.

c

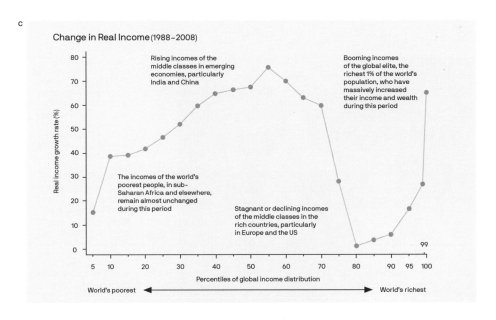

Change in Real Income (1988–2008)

Rising incomes of the middle classes in emerging economies, particularly India and China

Booming incomes of the global elite, the richest 1% of the world's population, who have massively increased their income and wealth during this period

The incomes of the world's poorest people, in sub-Saharan Africa and elsewhere, remain almost unchanged during this period

Stagnant or declining incomes of the middle classes in the rich countries, particularly in Europe and the US

Real income growth rate (%)

Percentiles of global income distribution

World's poorest ← → World's richest

All these activities, including others such as mining, logging and road-building through remote areas, have led to a major disruption of ecosystems. Deforestation and landscape changes are causing animals to lose habitats, with the result that species become crowded together and also come into greater contact with other animal species they have never been near before, including humans. In this disruption, pathogens that used to be held in check by forest ecologies, are now increasingly breaking free and crossing over into humans in a process known as 'zoonotic spillover'.

The US Center for Disease Control and Prevention estimates that 75% of new or emerging diseases that infect humans originate in animals, and in recent years there has been a worrying increase in such diseases, including Ebola, Zika, swine flu and diseases caused by coronaviruses, such as SARS in 2002 and COVID-19 in 2019–20.

While much production has shifted to developing countries, the overall control of production has mainly stayed with large companies with headquarters in the developed countries. These corporations have either set up subsidiaries in developing countries or formed complex networks of companies, called supply chains. In the process, large companies have expanded to become huge TNCs, overseeing a global production process of goods and food that organizes the work, and shapes the lives and livelihoods, of people in a huge number of different countries around the world. Today, there are more than 100,000 TNCs and they completely dominate world production and trade, accounting for around a third of world output and two-thirds of world trade.

A

A   Health workers carry the coffin of an Ebola victim in the Democratic Republic of the Congo. Ebola is a highly contagious viral disease that crossed from animals to humans in tropical Africa. The 2014–16 epidemic killed over 10,000 people and the disease is still spreading in some countries.
B   Container ships docked at the Port of Shanghai, China. Maritime transport accounts for around 4% of total greenhouse gas emissions. However, because these emissions mainly take place at sea, countries do not include them in their national totals and there is little effort at mitigation.

B

A **supply chain** is a network of companies that collaborate to make a product. The lead company, usually in a developed country, oversees product design and marketing, and sets the timetable and cost parameters. Other companies in the network, usually based in various developing countries, produce the item.

As production has globalized, international trade has increased as items produced in developing countries are frequently transported to developed countries for sale. In fact, it is not only the final products that move around the world in this way; raw materials and components are also traded between companies in different countries in complex supply chains in order to make the final item.

The container ships and aeroplanes that transport these items back and forth across the globe emit large amounts of carbon dioxide and other green-house gases. Rising levels of international trade therefore substantially contribute to climate change.

A

Much of contemporary international trade is 'arm's length trade' between two separate companies who negotiate price and terms according to the market. However, an increasing proportion of international trade – more than 30% – is now between two subsidiaries of the same TNC. In this 'intra-firm trade', one part of a global company is essentially trading with another part of the same company. This is not free trade, but a system through which a TNC can set the price and terms however they like. It provides a mechanism through which profits can be moved from one country to another without anyone outside the company knowing.

For example, imagine a TNC called CORP, which is headquartered in France and has two subsidiaries: the mining company CORP (Nigeria) and the consulting company CORP (Luxembourg). If CORP (Nigeria) buys advisory services from CORP (Luxembourg), the executives in the CORP headquarters in France can decide how much they should pay. Since this money will never leave the CORP corporation, they could choose to set the cost far higher than the actual market cost, and in this way covertly move money from Nigeria to Luxembourg. By shifting profits out of high tax jurisdictions into tax havens or low tax jurisdictions they can avoid paying taxes. This practice, known as 'transfer mispricing', makes it extremely difficult for states to collect tax from TNCs.

This is just one example of how TNCs manage to escape regulation in today's globalized system. The fact that, economically, TNCs are run as one global company, but are legally organized as a network of separate companies registered in different countries, makes it virtually impossible to effectively tax or regulate them. The TNC form has thus enabled large corporations to routinely escape both government oversight and social responsibility to pay taxes for the public good.

Many TNCs that operate in developing countries are in the extractive sector. This industry requires close regulation due to the huge potential environmental and safety hazards. However, these TNCs are so large and influential that weak developing countries do not have the power to hold them to account. Instead governments frequently collude with the corporations and assist them by resettling people away from land that has mining potential or turning a blind eye when pollution starts to spoil the environment and impact on the health and well being of local peoples. Bribery and corruption also play major roles in the relationship between TNCs and developing country governments. The overall result is that local and foreign elites get rich while peasants, indigenous communities and other rural people suffer.

The **extractive sector** consists of industries that extract and process raw materials from the earth. Major industries in the extractive sector include oil and gas and the mining of metals, diamonds and minerals.

A A protester throws fake money in a demonstration against tax havens. London, UK, 2016.
B Indigenous people from the Pataxo-Hahahae group look at the Paraopeba River full of toxic sludge after the collapse of a dam at an upstream iron-ore mine. Many rural people in developing countries first encounter 'globalization' when a TNC arrives near their community, takes their land to build a mine or drill for oil, and then pollutes the soil, air or water on which their lives depend.

A

TNCs have not only globalized their production systems, they have also globalized their sales and marketing. This means that very many of the same products, produced by the same corporations, are now on sale almost everywhere in the world.

Not only does this push out local businesses, but it also leads to a reduction in diversity and a homogenizing of consumption along the lines of Western or US 'consumer culture'. Whether you live in London, Chicago, Tokyo or Nairobi, you may well drink Coca-Cola, eat at McDonald's, watch the news on CNN, the BBC or Al Jazeera, listen to the same rock music, follow the same sporting events and view the same films. This is certainly not a total homogenization – differences in dress, food and cultural traditions, of course, persist – but among elites and middle classes in urban centres, the differences are getting much smaller.

B

In **consumer culture** constant advertising drives people to buy goods and services to project a certain lifestyle image, and shopping itself becomes a leisure activity.

A   A man stands outside
    a local shop advertising
    Coca-Cola, Mauritania.
B   An Orthodox priest sits
    in front of a shop made
    out of a shipping container
    emblazoned with Coca-Cola
    insignia, Ethiopia.

In the major cities of the world, an increasingly shared global cosmopolitan culture is developing. The same is less true among poorer people and in rural areas.

As many previously remote communities become connected to regional urban centres through new roads, they find their local economies are destroyed as young people migrate to the towns and subsidized foreign food items undermine local production. New products, from Madonna CDs and Barbie dolls to Rambo videos and pornography, arrive in local markets and upset cultural norms and behaviour. People become concerned that Western values, of individualism, consumerism and secularism, are undermining their own traditional value systems. They feel angry that their local cultures are being bulldozed by a Western culture that is being swept around the world by globalization.

A   Adverts in developing countries, such as this hoarding advertising a skin-whitening cream in Abidjan, Ivory Coast (above) and this display of skin-whitening products in Pakistan (below), urge people to make themselves 'more beautiful' by using chemicals to lighten their skin or hair or to 'correct' their dark eyes with blue contact lenses. People that do not conform to Western stereotypes often lose their self-esteem.

B   Traders at the Chicago Board Options Exchange, USA, (above) and at a brokerage house at Dhaka, Bangladesh (below). Contemporary globalization has initiated a process of 'financialization', in which financial markets, financial actors, financial institutions and financial motives now play a major role in the operation of domestic and international economies.

Continual bombardment by Western media and advertising leads people in many places to feel ashamed of their own culture and lifestyles. Satellite television now brings US adventure movies and sitcoms showing luxury lifestyles to the most remote parts of the world, making village life seem primitive and boring by contrast. Western media stereotypes are almost invariably based on an urban, blonde, blue-eyed model. If you are a farmer or are dark-skinned, you can quickly come to feel backward and inferior.

In some places people rally against the homogenizing forces of globalization. They place more emphasis on their local traditions or become more fundamentalist in their religious beliefs. In many parts of the world globalization has unintentionally catalysed a resurgence of religion in public life and an increase in inter-ethnic and inter-religious conflict.

Perhaps the most important feature of contemporary globalization is the globalization of financial markets.

When governments removed capital controls and deregulated financial markets, there was a huge increase in the volume of financial activity, as the ability to trade in different markets, combined with new technologies, led to new ways of making money on the financial markets. Because governments opted to retain control of their monetary policy and move to a system of floating exchange rates, a new kind of financial system emerged in which national currencies essentially compete against each other within the global market and their relative values go up and down accordingly. This has opened up a vast new area of financial activity, as currency speculators can now gamble on the behaviour of these different national currencies, trying to buy when they are low and sell when they are high. A whole raft of complex financial instruments has been created to meet the demands of this new type of financial activity, mainly in the form of highly risky 'derivatives', such as 'futures', 'options' and 'swaps'.

Derivatives are financial securities whose value is derived from that of an underlying group of assets, such as stocks, bonds, commodities, interest rates or currencies.

Futures are contracts to buy or sell an asset at a predetermined price on a specified date.

Options are contracts that give buyers the right, but not the obligation, to buy or sell an asset at a predetermined price on a specified date.

Swaps are contracts through which two parties exchange the cash flows or liabilities from two different financial instruments.

In **financial capitalism**, money is made mainly by trading or investing in currencies and financial products. A key activity is speculation, essentially gambling whether the value of a currency or financial product will rise or fall. It is sometimes referred to as 'casino capitalism'.

A **financial crash** happens when financial assets suddenly lose a large part of their nominal value and great amounts of financial wealth are instantly wiped off balance sheets. Major financial crashes have increased since the 1980s and include the New York stock market crash of 1987, the Asian financial crisis of 1997–98, and the US sub-prime mortgage crash of 2008.

Austerity is a set of political-economic policies that aim to reduce government budget deficits through spending cuts, tax increases or a combination of both.

In contemporary globalization, like never before, it is possible to make huge amounts of money by speculating, or gambling, on the financial markets. The size of the financial sector has now far outstripped the size of the 'real' productive economic sector, and today global finance is around 50 times bigger than world trade. More profit is made by trading and speculating in the financial markets than by producing goods and services in the real economy. The global economy has transitioned from industrial capitalism to a new system of **financial capitalism**.

Unregulated global financial markets have proved to be inherently unstable, and since the 1980s there has been a series of **financial crashes**. These crashes have ruined many livelihoods and ravaged millions of lives, contributing to increasing poverty and inequality.

A
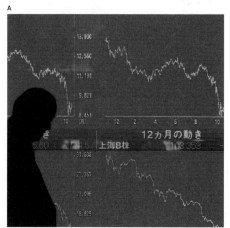

B

C

A   A stock price
indicator board
in October 2008
showing plunging
stock values.

B   Protestors
demonstrate behind
Richard Fuld, head
of the investment
bank Lehman
Brothers, which
collapsed in 2008
due to the sub-prime
mortgage crisis.

C   Satirical performance
art on Wall Street
during the 2008
financial crisis.
Three suited artists,
representing bankers
with briefcases full
of money, hold tin
cups for bailouts.

After the financial crash in 2008, Western governments used taxpayers money to bail out the big banks so that they would not collapse. This resulted in a severe lack of government funds for public expenditure, such as education, public health services and welfare, and thus the implementation of highly unpopular austerity policies. They also printed more money and put it in the financial markets, through a process called 'quantitative easing', in order to try to stimulate a resurgence of financial activity. Printing money usually results in inflation, but because policy-makers put this money into the financial sector and not into the real economy, it meant that they could stop a general inflation (and keep interest rates low) and only cause an inflation in asset prices. The result has been very good for wealthy people who own a lot of assets and property, but very bad for poor people who now have to pay higher rents.

The system of global finance and national level politics has also made it virtually impossible for governments to tax the wealthy. If capital can simply flow across borders, then the very wealthy will surely take it out of high taxation countries and place it instead in countries with low tax regimes. Consequently, states have had to compete against each other by lowering their rates of corporate taxation to try to stem such 'capital flight'.

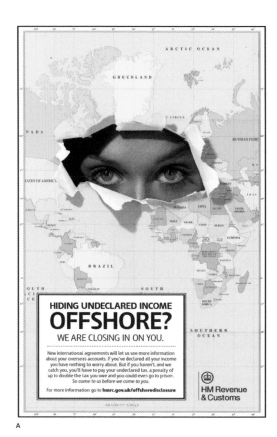

HIDING UNDECLARED INCOME
OFFSHORE?
WE ARE CLOSING IN ON YOU.

New international agreements will let us see more information about your overseas accounts. If you've declared all your income you have nothing to worry about. But if you haven't, and we catch you, you'll have to pay your undeclared tax, a penalty of up to double the tax you owe and you could even go to prison. *So come to us before we come to you.*

For more information go to **hmrc.gov.uk/offshoredisclosure**

HM Revenue & Customs

A

Tax haven is a term that was coined in the 1950s, but the concept actually originated in the late 19th century in the USA, where the state of New Jersey effectively became the world's first tax haven by easing its business registration and tax laws. Switzerland and Liechtenstein later copied the practice. In the 1950s and 1960s, new tax havens were established in British offshore territories such as Jersey, Guernsey and the Cayman Islands. Since the 1980s, the number of tax havens has soared to around 100, including places such as the Netherlands, Mauritius and Panama.

'Letterbox' companies are businesses that establish their legal domicile in a country with low tax rates with just a mailing address, while they conduct their actual commercial activities elsewhere.

The development of tax havens since the 1970s has made it even easier for global capital to avoid taxation anywhere.

Tax havens are states that choose to use three types of policies: low or zero taxation for non-residents, easy methods of business incorporation and legally protected secrecy. Wealthy individuals and TNCs can set up 'letterbox' companies in these jurisdictions in order to benefit from high levels of secrecy and avoid paying taxes. Tax havens now play a central role in today's globalized financial system. It has been estimated that over 50% of all the money in the world either resides in a tax haven or has passed through one, and that more than 30% of global foreign direct investment passes through a tax haven.

The fact that financial globalization has made it almost impossible to tax the rich has huge implications for everyone and for the societies in which we live.

It means that despite all the economic growth in the past few decades, much of this wealth is private, not public, and governments now have less money than they did before (relative to GDP, or gross domestic product). This has led to governments cutting public spending and implementing austerity policies. In developed countries, this has resulted in cuts to public health services and an eating away of the institutions of the welfare state. In developing countries, it has meant that there is insufficient public money to provide basic economic safety nets or to build schools, hospitals and the infrastructure necessary for development.

The consequences of this lack of investment in public health have been laid starkly bare during the COVID-19 global pandemic in 2020, in which hospitals around the world were overwhelmed and doctors had to choose which patients to save with the limited medical equipment available.

A Poster from a 2014 UK HMRC campaign targeting taxpayers with money hidden in offshore accounts.

B A doctor attends to patients in intensive care in the COVID-19 ward of the Maria Pia Hospital in Turin, Italy, April 2020. The Piedmont region around the city of Turin was the second worst hit in Italy, after Lombardy, with over 29,000 deaths.

C Deaths from COVID-19 in New York, USA, overwhelmed the city's permanent morgues and filled hospital storage spaces to capacity. Hospital staff in Brooklyn are here seen moving dead bodies to a refrigerated truck, which is serving as a temporary morgue.

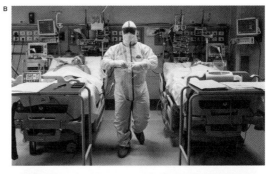

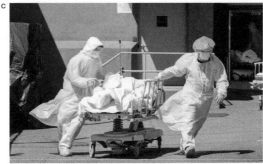

A

The major fall in tax incomes has been a significant driver in most governments taking larger loans and getting deeper and deeper into debt. This rise in sovereign debt is very important for two major reasons. First, when governments are in debt, it is citizens who are paying the interest on this debt through their tax payments, and this can amount to billions of dollars every year.

For example, in 2018 the UK's national debt was just over £1.7 trillion and its interest payment for the year was £48 billion. That means that £48 billion, around 8% of the money that people paid in taxes, was used to pay interest to financial creditors rather than to create jobs, build infrastructure or provide public services. Just about every country, large and small, has billions or trillions of dollars of sovereign debt. In 2018 this added up to a total of more than $50 trillion. The result is that every year hundreds of billions of dollars of tax-payers money flow into the financial sector as interest payments, making profits for creditors rather than providing public services or funding welfare states. In 2020, as governments round the world borrow large sums of money to pay for the costs of the COVID-19 pandemic, sovereign debt is poised to soar even more.

Developing countries find that their debts tend to grow faster due to higher interest rates, falling local currency values and the low price of commodity exports on which most of their economies rely, such that their levels of sovereign

B

debt quickly become unsustainable. Many developing country governments pay around 14% of their income in interest to foreign creditors. In some countries the amounts are even higher, reaching 24.5% in Sri Lanka and 42.4% in Ghana. In 2017 Angola paid a staggering 55.4% of its national revenue to service foreign debts. Money that could have gone towards basic development activities was instead siphoned off as interest payments to wealthy overseas creditors, making it virtually impossible for these countries to develop their own economies and societies.

Sovereign debt is the amount of money a national government owes to its creditors.

The second reason that rising government debt is important is because, as we saw in Chapter 1, indebted countries risk losing their sovereignty to make their own policy decisions, as creditors can tie all sorts of policy conditions to their loans.

A   A German national debt clock, on a building in Berlin, 2009.

B   The US national debt clock, installed in 1989, was the first debt clock. It is located in an alley between West 42nd St and West 43rd St. The displayed debt is as of 23 March 2018.

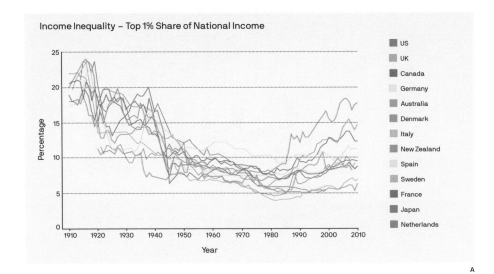

Income Inequality – Top 1% Share of National Income

Legend: US, UK, Canada, Germany, Australia, Denmark, Italy, New Zealand, Spain, Sweden, France, Japan, Netherlands

Y-axis: Percentage (0, 5, 10, 15, 20, 25)
X-axis: Year (1910, 1920, 1930, 1940, 1950, 1960, 1970, 1980, 1990, 2000, 2010)

A

When governments are in debt, they are increasingly subservient to the wishes of the IMF and other creditors, who force them to follow neoliberal policies. Since the 1970s, private credit rating agencies have emerged, which rate countries according to how well their policies follow neoliberal orthodoxy. The interest rate on loans given to governments is then determined by these ratings, so that loans become more expensive if governments do not toe the line and implement the 'right' policies. With sovereign debt at an all-time high, most governments have little choice but to implement neoliberal policies, even if their citizens want something else. Political scientist Stephen Gill has called this process 'disciplinary neoliberalism'.

Policies that please the credit rating agencies are generally those that prioritize the payment of sovereign debt. However, these policies are often detrimental to ordinary people. For example, the Mexican government had to abandon an agricultural reform designed to expand medium-sized farming for local consumption goods, which would have been beneficial to many of its citizens, and instead revert to large-scale production of luxury export crops in order to earn dollars to service the country's debt. Disciplinary neoliberalism, therefore, often comes into conflict with national democracy.

Taken altogether, the economic changes of contemporary globalization have led to a huge increase in economic inequality in just about every country in the world.

French economist Thomas Piketty has become famous for his scrupulously detailed work showing how income inequality has increased in most countries since the 1970s. Wealth inequality has increased even more. Research by Oxfam shows that the world's 26 richest individuals now own as much wealth as the poorest half of the global population. In 2018, billionaires grew their combined fortunes by $2.5 billion a day, while the relative wealth of the world's poorest 3.8 billion people declined by $500 million a day.

While global wealth has soared, more than half of the world's population continue to live in abject poverty. Hundreds of millions of people lack access to sufficient food, to clean drinking water or to basic medicines, and millions of adults and children die every year from preventable diseases, such as diarrhoea and pneumonia.

B

A   A graph of income
     inequality trends
     in several countries,
     based on data from
     Thomas Piketty's book
     *Capital in the Twenty-
     First Century* (2013).
     It shows the decline
     in income inequality
     between 1900 and
     1980, followed by a
     sharp increase from
     1980 to the present.
B   Children scavenge
     in a rubbish dump in
     Freetown, Sierra Leone,
     2018. The United Nations
     Development Programme
     (UNDP) estimates that
     50% of the 1.3 billion
     people who live in
     poverty are children.

A

Even in rich countries, such as Britain, there has been an increase in poverty rates, homelessness rates and the use of food banks. Not only are the poor suffering, but increasingly the middle classes are seeing a decline in their living standards and the younger generation are no longer able to aspire to many of the things that their parents took for granted, such as a having a steady job and owning a home. Meanwhile, the elite have got richer and the number of billionaires has increased.

A   Rough sleepers in
     London. Rates of
     homelessness have
     been rising in many
     countries since 2008.
B   American billionaire
     Christopher Forbes.
     Since 2008 the
     number of billionaires
     has doubled from
     1,125 to 2,208.
     Economic inequality
     during contemporary
     globalization has
     returned to the high
     levels that were
     experienced during
     the first era of
     globalization.

How has it been possible to bring about these changes in democratic states? How have governments been able to ignore the suffering of ordinary people? Why have the population not voted for alternatives?

B

The answer is that since the 1980s there has been a process of economic de-democratization taking place in most countries.

While the structures of democracy are still in place, with political parties and elections, and so on, people's ability to influence economic policy through their votes has been much diminished. Democracy has been hollowed out. Political scientist Colin Crouch has called this situation 'post-democracy'.

De-democratization can take many forms.

One has been to quietly remove particular areas of economic policy-making from government oversight and thus democratic control. The best-known example is the increasing separation of central banks from political supervision.

Since the mid-1990s, the global economic policy consensus has been that central banks should be 'independent'. Now, being independent might sound good, but what it actually means is that central banks, and therefore monetary policy, are insulated from political control and thus democratic reach. As discussed in Chapter 1, monetary policy is very important and inherently political, because it can be set in ways that tend to benefit global financial markets or the ordinary people in a country. If monetary policy is removed from democratic influence, it becomes far easier for it to be set in favour of global financial elites.

A

Mr. M... rberg

Bilateral investment treaties (BITS) are agreements signed between two states that establish the terms and conditions for private investment by nationals and companies of one state in the other.

A   Facebook CEO Mark Zuckerberg testifying at a US Senate hearing, 2018. Governments and elites have long sought to control the media in order to influence what voters think. Today they do so in ever deeper ways with new technologies such as Facebook, computer algorithms and AI.

B   Protesters march in New Delhi, India, 2012, against a proposed EU–India bilateral trade and investment agreement, claiming it will negatively impact the supply of affordable medicines. Negotiations collapsed in 2013.

B

Another way that economic policy-making has been taken out of democratic control is through terms that are written into new-style trade and investment agreements, which have been increasingly developed since the 1970s. These include thousands of bilateral investment treaties (BITs), and also agreements between a group of countries or regions. These treaties are generally negotiated in secret without the democratic involvement of parliament or the people.

A standard feature of these agreements is a clause that states that the government of the country receiving the investment cannot make any policy changes, now or in the future, which might lead to a loss of 'expected profits' for the investor. Thus, for example, if the people vote in a new government that promises to raise taxes to fund public spending or to change pollution laws to better protect the environment, and these changes lead to the investor making a little less profit, then the investor can sue the government.

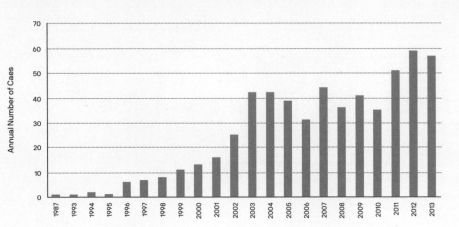

A

These cases are known as investor state dispute settlements (ISDSs) and they are heard in private arbitration panels, not in public courts. Many such cases have taken place and have resulted in governments having to pay hundreds of millions of dollars of taxpayers' money to investors, as well as millions more dollars in legal fees.

A   This graph produced by the United Nations Conference on Trade and Development (UNCTAD) shows a marked increase in the number of ISDS cases during the 2000s. Many fear a possible surge in cases after the COVID-19 pandemic as TNCs sue governments for loss of expected profit due to lockdown policies.

B   Aerial view of protests against rising inequality and the high cost of living in Santiago, Chile, 2019.

For example, in the 1990s, Argentina privatized many of its public services, including water and electricity. The private companies that took over these services put up the prices. In 2001, Argentina's economy fell into recession and there was terrible hyperinflation and a major loss of jobs, leading to widespread suffering and poverty. People took to the streets in desperation, calling for the government to do something. In this crisis situation, the government decided to freeze utility prices so that they would remain affordable to people. In response, it was hit by more than 40 lawsuits from the foreign companies, including Anglian Water (Britain), Suez and Vivendi (France) and Sociedad General de Aguas de Barcelona (Spain). The ISDS tribunal concluded that the Argentinian government had breached the terms of the investment treaties and ordered it to pay a total of $980 million.

The fear of similar lawsuits now leads many governments to simply refrain from making any policy changes that may trigger such cases. Thus, the decisions of current governments are being locked in for the future, restricting the democratic ability of future generations.

For all these reasons, and others, citizens are finding that it makes little difference who they vote for, because most economic policies have essentially already been decided and bracketed off from democratic input. This is why in many countries centre-right and centre-left political parties look increasingly the same.

As predicted by Rodrik's open polity trilemma, economic globalization has led to a massive reduction in democracy. In frustration, people have started to turn to populist politicians and to take to the streets.

B

3. The Anti-Globalization Backlash

A

With the recent rise of nationalism and populism in Europe and North America, including the election of Donald Trump as president of the USA and Britain's decision to leave the European Union, a new backlash against globalization appears to be taking place. In fact, resistance to globalization started in the 1980s with waves of anti-IMF protests.

Populism is a political philosophy that pits a virtuous and homogeneous 'people' against a set of elites or dangerous 'others', who are depicted as depriving the 'people' of their rights, prosperity, or identity.

Discontent with globalization has increased ever since, as it has affected more and more people around the world. While in the early years austerity policies were mainly imposed on developing countries, since the financial crash in 2008 they have increasingly been forced on developed countries as well. In each case, the results are the same: declining public services, higher cost of living and increased poverty and inequality.

CHAPTER 3

B

A   Brexit supporters wave British Union Jack flags at a Brexit Celebration party in Warrington, UK, on 31 January 2020, the day that the UK formally left the EU.
B   Donald Trump supporters at the President's 'Keep America Great' campaign rally at BancorpSouth Arena, Tupelo, Mississippi, November 2019.

Anti-globalization sentiment that started in developing countries has now also spread to developed countries.

In the 1980s high oil prices, rising inflation and collapsing commodity prices caused loans taken out by developing countries in the 1960s to spiral into huge debts, which jeopardized many economies. Countries had to ask the IMF for bailout loans and in exchange were forced to open their borders to global capital, re-orient their economies to focus on production for export, and implement austerity policies such as ending food and fuel subsidies. In most cases, these young countries were not ready to integrate into the global economy and instead needed protections in order to grow their own industries.

The impact, therefore, was dramatic. Prices of essential goods skyrocketed, incomes dwindled, jobs disappeared, services were cut and many people struggled to make ends meet. The effects were similar across a wide range of countries that implemented similar reforms. Throughout the developing world, most people suffered a drastic fall in their material standard of living and poverty soared. In Latin America, for example, the poverty rate increased from 32% in 1980 to 39% in 1985, while in sub-Saharan Africa per capita incomes dropped by 21% between 1981 and 1989.

A

B

A   A protester in Manila, Philippines, 1997, sets fire to effigies of representatives of the IMF-World Bank during a demonstration against IMF policies to privatize the state-owned water system.

B   Graffiti on a wall in Port-au-Prince, Haiti, 1995, changing the meaning of the acronym IMF (or in French, FMI, Fond Monétaire International) to 'Famine, Misery, Injustice', after the IMF forced the Haitian government to implement structural adjustment reforms and to privatize state-owned utilities despite widespread public opposition.

C   Parade of the Zapatista Army of National Liberation, Mexico, 1994. The Zapatistas fought for autonomy and control over land and local resources for indigenous peoples. They were one of the first popular movements to recognize neoliberalism as a dangerous new stage of global capitalism and launched their uprising on the day that Mexico signed the North America Free Trade Agreement (NAFTA).

Social movements are purposeful, organized groups working to promote social change. They are a form of informal, non-institutional, civilian-based collective action, which often emerges in response to situations of inequality, oppression or injustice.

c

This led to anti-IMF protests in numerous countries in the developing world. During the 1980s and 1990s, there were general strikes in Peru, Bolivia and India, food riots in Morocco, Brazil and Haiti, and huge demonstrations in dozens of other countries from Argentina to Paraguay, Malawi to Zambia, Jordan to Tunisia. In each case, tens of thousands, sometimes hundreds of thousands, of people came out onto the streets in indignation. Protesters were angry at the price rises of basic essentials, particularly bread and fuel, and also outraged that the IMF could force their governments to make these changes.

As globalization began to affect the lives of more and more people in the developing countries, social movements began to emerge as peasants, women, indigenous groups, landless farmers and others started to organize in order to resist. One of these movements, the Zapatista Army of National Liberation, a grassroots movement of impoverished indigenous people from the Mexican Chiapas, saw that the problems they were facing were not just caused by the particular policies of the Mexican government, but were also due to the evolving global system. And they realized that the problems faced by many social movements around the world were caused by these same global dynamics. In 1996, using the newly emerging technology of email, its activists reached out to similar movements in other countries and invited them to an international meeting. Over 6,000 people from more than 40 countries attended, including groups such as the Karnataka State Farmers Union from India, which had been struggling against foreign agri-business TNCs, the U'wa indigenous people of Colombia who were resisting foreign oil companies from drilling in their ancestral homeland, and the Landless Workers Movement of Brazil, who were calling for land reform and redistribution. This meeting led to the formation of one of the first global protest networks: Peoples Global Action (PGA).

As these groups began to conclude that increasing economic globalization was the cause of many of their problems, they started to organize a series of protests against the international institutions that seemed to run the global economy.

In 1999 the Direct Action Network, a North American network linked to the PGA, coordinated a number of huge demonstrations against the World Trade Organization. As the WTO met in Seattle to discuss further integration of the world's economies through reductions in trade barriers and other neoliberal economic measures, some 40,000 protestors took to the streets to demonstrate against these activities. They demanded a globalization that would benefit everyone on the planet, not just the wealthy elite.

A

A Demonstration in Seattle against the World Trade Organization, December, 1999. Protesters used a variety of creative techniques, including large puppets, street theatre, sit-ins, and locking themselves to metal pipes in strategic locations.

B Women and children washing clothes in polluted water under an oil pipeline in the Amazon forest, Ecuador. Oil drilling in the Amazon has huge environmental impacts: toxic wastewater leaches into the soil and rivers, and there are frequent oil spills from pipelines.

C Waorani people celebrate a court ruling in favour of the group's legal challenge to the government's move to auction off their ancestral lands for oil exploration, Puvo, Ecuador, 2019. The judges ruled that land concessions could not be given without the free, prior, and informed consent of the Waorani people themselves.

B

C

The protestors took control of downtown Seattle and prevented the WTO opening ceremony from taking place. In response, the police used pepper spray, tear gas and rubber bullets in their efforts to disperse the crowds. Some protesters responded in kind by throwing sticks and water bottles. The 'battle of Seattle' gained widespread media coverage and the protesters became known as the 'anti-globalization movement'.

After Seattle, the anti-globalization movement gained substantial momentum and increased its activities at both the global and local level. Over the next few years, large protests were organized outside nearly every meeting of the World Bank, IMF and WTO as protesters demanded a different kind of globalization and more accountability from these opaque organizations. At the local level, protests took place in many countries, including fights against water privatization in Bolivia and South Africa, resistance to the development of hydroelectric dams in rural India, and struggles to secure access to low-cost generic AIDS drugs in Africa.

The **World Social Forum (WSF)** is an annual meeting of NGOs and social movements seeking to develop alternatives to neoliberalism and corporate globalization.

A   Attendees of the 2009 World Social Forum in Belem, Brazil, hold up a huge model of the earth.

B   Aerial view of a protest against the deforestation of the Amazon during the 2009 World Social Forum. Around 1,000 protesters form the shape of a man holding a bow and arrow and the words 'Salvea Amazonas' ('Save the Amazon').

A

The movement was not against globalization per se, but rather against the specific form of neoliberal globalization, or corporate globalization, that was taking place. Many of its activists preferred other names, such as the 'alter-globalization movement', the 'anti-corporate globalization movement' or the 'global justice movement'. They cried, 'Our world is not for sale,' and rallied together under the slogan 'Another world is possible'.

In 2001, activists came together and created a forum in which the various movements could discuss what this other world might look like. The first meeting of the World Social Forum (WSF) was held in Porto Alegre, Brazil, and attracted some 12,000 participants. Since then, the WSF has been institutionalized as a regular event, taking place almost every year in different countries and at its peak drawing crowds of more than 100,000.

It provides a space for local and national social movements to network, learn from each other and discuss different ideas about how to create a better globalization – what many activists like to call 'globalization from below'.

Participants are very diverse and come with different ideas and agendas, speak different languages and have different cultural traditions. They include trade unionists, environmentalists, feminists, anarchists, land rights and indigenous rights activists, civil rights and human rights activists, anti-sweatshop campaigners and many more. Over the years, the WSF has helped to build mutual understanding and trust between these diverse groups and to foster creative ideas and debate.

B

However, the WSF was designed as a venue for discussion, not as a space for political organizing. It is based on 'open space' processes and participatory democracy, such that there are no leaders, no one represents anyone else and participants are not pressured to reach agreement with others. While this 'horizontality' is highly democratic and ensures that all voices are heard, it has stopped the movement from coalescing into an organized political force that could press for change.

A   Graffiti in Cairo, Egypt, during the Arab Spring. The Arabic text says that the army uses the blood of the Egyptian people and elections to get power.

B   Egyptians in Tahrir Square, Cairo, during the largest protest of the Arab Spring. Within two weeks the demonstrations led to the resignation of President Hosni Murbarak and the end of his 30-year rule.

Furthermore, the fear of oppression in organized structures, what activists call 'verticality', has made participants shy away from thinking how to reform global structures, such as the UN or WTO, or how to create new global structures that could lead to social change and global justice. Instead, most of the solutions offered by WSF participants have been small scale and localized, practised by a particular group here or there. For these and other reasons, the movement lost momentum.

A

B

The next wave of protest came in the years after the 2008 financial crisis.

To get the economy going again, central banks in the USA and Europe injected more money into the economy via quantitative easing. This fuelled a wave of speculation in commodities markets, which stoked inflation in food prices around the globe. This time, it was the Arab world that burst into protest. The rise in food prices heightened long-standing concerns over increasing poverty and inequality and intensified anger at other grievances, such as political repression, police brutality and corruption. On 17 December 2010, fruit seller Mohamed Bouazizi lit a match and set himself on fire, thus sparking the Tunisian revolution and a series of national uprisings across the Middle East known as the 'Arab Spring'.

A core demand in these protests was for greater democratic representation, as people wanted their governments to take back control of their economic policies and to allow people to live according to their own cultural values. The uprisings toppled leaders in Tunisia, Egypt, Yemen and Libya, brought about reforms in Morocco and Algeria or were violently crushed, as in Bahrain and Syria.

Another wave of major protests erupted across Europe and the USA. In contrast to the anti-globalization demonstrations of the late 1990s, which mainly focused on the injustices suffered by those in developing countries, these protests concentrated for the first time on the injustices in developed countries. In response to the 2008 financial crisis, many governments had imposed strict austerity policies, which led to increasing unemployment, falling wages, and reductions in public services. The cuts went so deep that even the middle class felt the pain. Many found themselves saddled with debt and sliding into poverty. Young people struggled to find employment and even university graduates could no longer count on a good job and a comfortable standard of living. Anger and confusion at this state of affairs led conventional mainstream people to join more radical activists on the streets.

A

A   Protests in 2011 in Madrid, Spain, (top left), New York, USA, (top right), Berlin, Germany, (bottom left) and Rio de Janeiro, Brazil, (bottom right). Protesters around the world adopted similar symbols and slogans, and used tent occupations to take over public spaces.

B   A banner at the Occupy London tent camp in Finsbury Park, UK, 2011.

In May 2011 the Spanish filled city squares with the *Indignados* or 15M (15 May) protests, and in July Israelis took to the streets in social justice protests, known as J14 (July 14). In September, the Occupy Wall Street movement burst onto the streets of New York, taking over Zuccotti Park, and other 'occupations' soon followed in cities all over the USA and Europe and as far afield as Australia, Hong Kong and South Africa.

While these protest movements used many of the same organizing styles as the anti-globalization movement, such as leaderless participatory democracy, horizontalism and a carnivalesque atmosphere, the protesters this time focused on national level problems and called for their national governments to solve them. When asked to formulate their demands, most of these movements failed to do so. They were demonstrating *against* the rising cost of living, increasing economic inequality and the erosion of democracy. They were protesting against the current system of unregulated financial globalization, but they did not have a clear idea of what they were protesting *for*.

A

A   Catholic faithful demonstrate against rising fuel prices and IMF policies in a silent and non-violent march in Port-au-Prince, Haiti, October 2019.

B   *Gilets jaunes* protesters near Place de la Bastille (left) and in front of the Arc of Triomphe (right) in Paris, France, 2019.

In recent years, the anti-globalization backlash has been gathering momentum. In 2018 and 2019, austerity policies removing food and fuel subsidies triggered another wave of anti-IMF protests in many countries, including Ecuador, Haiti, Chile, Jordan, Lebanon, Sudan and Zimbabwe.

In 2018, the *gilets jaunes* (yellow vests) movement in France was triggered by a rise in fuel taxes, and later broadened into a more general protest against austerity measures and tax reforms, which protesters argued were disproportionately hurting the working and middle classes and those living in rural areas. In November 2018, more than 300,000 people donned the yellow high-visibility vests that French law requires all motorists to keep in their vehicles and took to the streets to gridlock France's road network. Demonstrations and roadblocks brought the nation to a halt.

However, in most democratic countries, protest has now started to take a different form: it has moved from the streets to the ballot box as people have sought to bring about change by turning to populist parties that pit 'the people' against various others.

In many countries, there has been a rise in both right-wing and left-wing populism. Broadly speaking, right-wing populists have been more successful in Northern Europe and the USA, while left-wing populists have gained more support in Southern Europe and Latin America.

B

A

A   Political satire on a float at the Rose Monday carnival in Düsseldorf, Germany, with huge puppets of 'right-wing dictators' Viktor Orbán (right) and Jaroslaw Kaczynski (left), 2018.

B   The meeting of two right-wing populist leaders: Brazil's Jair Bolsonaro (left) shakes hands with India's Narendra Modi (right), New Delhi, 2020.

Right-wing populist parties in Europe include the Freedom Party of Austria, National Rally (France), Alternative for Germany, the League (Italy), Vox (Spain), United Kingdom Independence Party, the Danish People's Party, the Finns Party (Finland), Sweden Democrats, the Conservative People's Party of Estonia, the Slovenian Democratic Party, Law and Justice (Poland) and the Hungarian Civic Alliance.

Right-wing populists present globalization as a worldwide conspiracy against national identity, Western culture or the white man, and then offer a solution in the form of 'de-globalization', by tightening borders and blocking immigration. They emphasize a cultural cleavage between the national, ethnic, religious or cultural identity of 'the people' and outside groups, such as immigrants or refugees who, they claim, pose a threat to the popular culture.

Left-wing populists, in contrast, present globalization as a movement of the bankers and the financial elites against 'the people', and then suggest solutions such as renegotiating austerity measures and increasing public spending. They emphasize an economic cleavage between the elites who control the economy and the lower income groups who lack access to power. Like the anti-globalization movement, they are not against globalization per se, but against the current form of neoliberal globalization. Implicitly, they seek an alternative form of globalization, although during elections they mainly emphasize progressive national policies.

B

Right-wing populist parties emerged rapidly in many European countries, including Austria, France, Germany, Italy, Spain, Denmark, Finland, Sweden, Estonia and Slovenia. In Poland and Hungary, right-wing populist parties have come to power, in the form of Jarosław Kaczyński's (b. 1949) Law and Justice party and Viktor Orbán's (b. 1963) Hungarian Civic Alliance. Right-wing populists have also come to power in Turkey, India, Brazil and elsewhere.

But the most surprising examples of right-wing populism came to the fore in 2016 in two major shocks: the election of Donald Trump as president of the USA, and the vote of the British public to leave the EU.

Trump won the election on a strongly anti-globalist platform, promising to 'make America great again' by slowing migration, implementing protectionist economic policies and withdrawing from international obligations. His campaign demonized Mexican immigrants, Muslim refugees and other racial and ethnic minorities. His impulsive and no-holds-barred campaign style made him appear 'a man of the people', despite being a billionaire.

A   Boris Johnson, then
    Mayor of London,
    speaks at the launch
    of the 'Vote Leave'
    campaign, May 2016.
B   Donald Trump won
    the 2016 US election
    even though only
    46% of voters chose
    him compared to
    the 48% who voted
    for Hillary Clinton.
    This is because US
    presidential elections
    are not based on
    a direct vote, but on
    a system of 'electoral
    colleges' which are
    distributed among
    states, with a bias
    in favour of less
    populous states.
    The upper map shows
    the results of the
    election by state and
    gives the impression
    that the Republicans
    won by a wide margin.
    In the lower map
    the sizes of states
    have been rescaled
    according to their
    population, showing
    that the vote was
    actually very close.

The campaign for Britain to leave the EU, or 'Brexit', was fuelled by Nigel Farage (b. 1964), and his right-wing populist United Kingdom Independence Party (UKIP). The Brexiters portrayed the EU as an undemocratic organization that undermined British democracy by imposing the rule of unelected technocrats in Brussels on the British people. They called for Britain to 'regain its sovereignty' by withdrawing from the EU. Most insistently, they argued that Britain should take control of its borders and reduce the inflow of immigrants, especially those from Muslim or other ethnic minority backgrounds, who they claimed were overwhelming the country.

In both cases, the vote was for nationalism and against globalization.

A

Brexit is an abbreviation for 'British exit', and refers to Britain leaving the EU. The question of whether Britain should leave the EU was put to the population in a referendum on 23 June 2016, and a small majority (52%) voted in favour. Britain eventually left the EU on 31 January 2020.

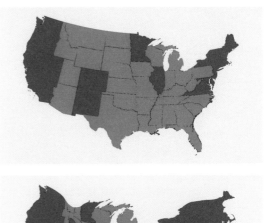

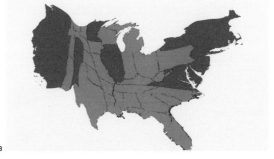

B

Supporters were primarily from rural communities and lower socio-economic groups, who had been suffering economically due to job losses and price rises caused by globalization, or older white people with more nationalist and conservative views, who felt that their culture and way of life were being threatened by ethnic or racial 'others' and, in the USA, by what they perceived to be overly liberal policies towards women and the LGBT community.

Left-wing populism, in contrast, gained more support in Latin America and Southern Europe. During the first decade of the 2000s, left-wing populists came to power in many Latin American countries, in what was called the 'pink tide'.

Left-wing populist parties
in Europe include Podemos (Spain), Left Bloc (Portugal), Syriza (Greece), Untamed France, the Party of Democratic Socialism (Germany) and the Socialist Party (the Netherlands). Jeremy Corbyn took Britain's Labour Party in a populist direction, while Bernie Sanders tried to do the same with the US Democratic Party.

A A campaign poster for Evo Morales on the outskirts of La Paz, Bolivia, saying 'Evo and the people. Secure future', October 2019.
B A poster in support of Venezuelan President Hugo Chavez reads 'We will triumph', 2006.
C Over 150,000 Podemos supporters demonstrate against austerity at Puerta del Sol in Madrid, Spain, January 2015.

In different ways, and to varying extents – Néstor (1950–2010) and Cristina (b. 1953) Kirchner in Argentina, Evo Morales (b. 1959) in Bolivia, Luiz Inácio Lula da Silva (b. 1945) in Brazil, Rafael Correa (b. 1963) in Ecuador and Hugo Chávez (1954–2013) in Venezuela – all sought to partially disengage their countries from the global economy and from what they perceived to be the imperialist machinations of the international financial institutions.

For example, Morales removed Bolivia from the World Bank's International Centre for the Settlement of Investment Disputes (an ISDS arbitration system), pulled out of BITs and 'de-dollarized' the economy. In this way, he neutralized much of the power of foreign capital and TNCs, was able to use monetary policy to benefit Bolivians rather than international capital, and in general brought economic policy under national control. With the political freedom that this generated, he started a programme of massive public investment and redistribution of wealth, paid for by a combination of nationalization of major industries and higher rates of corporate taxation.

The minimum monthly wage was increased threefold, social transfer payments were given to millions of poorer Bolivians and huge changes were made to the education system in order to bring more people into full-time education. The results were impressive. The country's economy grew at a steady 4.9% per year. Real per capita GDP increased by more than 50% over 13 years. And poverty fell from 60% in 2006 to 35% in 2017.

In Europe, left-wing populist parties have emerged in Spain, Portugal, Greece, France, Germany and the Netherlands. The most well-known are Syriza, which came to power in Greece in 2015 and Podemos, which emerged as a major political force in Spain in the same year. Both parties promised to stop austerity and reduce inequality and unemployment. However, while these problems were largely caused by globalization and exacerbated by European integration, these parties did not have a clear stance on how they would deal with dynamics beyond the nation state. Whilst they both initially sought to build a progressive alliance to change the terms of European integration and to create an 'Alternative Europe', they both quickly fell back into a kind of 'social nationalism', attempting to use the traditional left-wing tools to solve internal problems.

c

However, these types of traditional left-wing policies are no longer possible in the context of globalization, in which governments have to follow the policies called for by their creditors rather than by their electorate. This was clearly shown in the case of Greece.

In 2015, Greece found itself in a terrible debt crisis. The European Commission, European Central Bank and IMF proposed to offer loans to bail out the country, but these loans came with the condition that the Greek government impose severe austerity policies. The left-wing Syriza government had been elected on a platform of stopping austerity and cracking down on oligarchs and thus was reluctant to accept these terms. It called a referendum to put the question to the people. A clear majority of 61% rejected the austerity conditions of the bailout. Syriza tried to renegotiate the terms of the loan and to reduce the austerity measures, but the creditors would not budge. Thus, Syriza found itself with the choice of accepting the bailout or risking the collapse of Greece's banking sector, uncontrollable inflation and possibly Greece's exit from the EU. Despite the people's vote, Syriza turned to the EU only three days later to ask for a $59 billion loan and agreed to implement the required austerity policies.

The lack of viable policy alternatives to globalization is one of the reasons that the populist left has been less successful to date than the populist right in Europe and the USA.

A

A A banner outside the Greek parliament shows a wall, with all the austerity measures written on it, being smashed by a wrecking ball that says 'Oxi' ('No'), Syntagma Square, Athens, Greece, July 2015. Thousands of Greek citizens demonstrated outside the parliament calling on the government to honour the result of the referendum.

B Congresswoman Alexandria Ocasio-Cortez, also known as AOC, endorses 2020 Democratic presidential candidate Bernie Sanders at a campaign rally in New York, USA, October 2019.

C US President Donald Trump speaks at a 'Keep America Great' campaign rally in Las Vegas, USA, February 2020.

B

C

The anti-globalization backlash is thus not new. It has travelled around the world from the developing countries to the developed countries, as neoliberal globalization and financial crashes have led to debt and austerity policies in a growing number of countries. There is a striking similarity across all countries in the debt–austerity–protest cycle, as neoliberal globalization allows elites to suck wealth out of societies and economies around the world.

Now that the backlash is coming from the rich and powerful countries, who themselves are responsible for globalization, people are beginning to wonder if the world has reached a tipping point. With the COVID-19 pandemic leading to closed borders and rising xenophobia, and with right-wing populist leaders in power in the US and several other countries, is contemporary globalization finally over? Are we about to enter a new phase of nationalism? Or can globalization be transformed so that it brings increased opportunities, more responsible joined-up thinking on climate change and health, and prosperity for everyone?

4. Is Another Globalization Possible?

A   A labourer loads coal into a furnace in a steel factory in China, November 2016. China's rapid industrialization has led to it being the country with the largest carbon emissions. This is partly driven by the many foreign companies that have relocated to China because of its weak environmental regulation, using it as a kind of 'pollution haven'.

B   A worker in a cobalt mine in the Democratic Republic of the Congo, June 2016. Most of the world's cobalt comes from DRC, where large TNCs from Europe, China and elsewhere run mines to supply global tech companies with the material for use in rechargeable lithium-ion batteries for computers, smart phones and electric cars. While global demand has soared, mines are very poorly regulated and have been linked to human rights abuses, dangerous conditions and child labour.

Many scholars and commentators argue that globalization is now at a critical point.

While some believe that it can continue in more or less its present configuration for at least another 20 to 30 years, others are claiming that it has already gone into reverse. Others still are arguing that if globalization is to succeed then it must radically transform so that it works for the benefit of everyone.

They claim that other kinds of globalization are possible.

B

Dani Rodrik's open polity trilemma (see p.31) highlighted the tensions between national sovereignty, democracy and economic globalization and showed how it was only ever possible to have two out of the three. This analytic framework can be helpful in thinking about the shape of possible future world orders.

According to the trilemma, there are essentially three options:

de-democratization
globalization plus national sovereignty, without democracy;

de-globalization
national sovereignty plus democracy, without globalization;

de-nationalism
globalization plus democracy, without national sovereignty.

The de-democratization option represents the continuation of the globalization process that has been developing since the 1980s, with increasing economic globalization alongside national sovereignty, but with decreasing democracy.

This configuration leads to an erosion of democracy as governments find themselves bound in various ways to create policies that will attract global capital and please the capital markets. These policies are often unpopular with citizens because they tend to redistribute wealth from the poor to the rich, so governments find ways to remove economic matters from democratic control. This process has already led to significant de-democratization and if it continues it may lead to an even more total erosion of our national democracy and a move towards a world ruled by the uncontrolled might of money, facilitated by algorithms, artificial intelligence and undemocratic forms of global governance.

Several scholars and commentators believe that this scenario will continue, at least for the next few decades. Some, such as Susan Lund, think that globalization will remain in more or less its current configuration, despite recent setbacks; others, including Martin Jacques, suggest that it is already undergoing a significant reshaping as China emerges as a major player.

Since 2000, China has risen to be a major economic power, challenging US hegemony. When China entered the WTO in 2001, its share of world trade was only one-fifth of that of the USA, but in recent years it has overtaken the USA to become the dominant player in world trade. While US-centred international trade may be declining, other trends suggest that a new wave of China-centred international trade is emerging, driven in part by China's enormous Belt and Road Initiative. While the USA is pulling out of international agreements, such as the Paris Agreement on climate change, and reducing its role in international organizations such as the UN, China is becoming increasingly involved in processes of global governance and China's president, Xi Jinping (b. 1953), has said that his country will step forward and assume the leadership of 21st-century globalization.

But whether economic globalization is led by the USA or by China, if we continue to have economic globalization and national sovereignty then democracy must fall away.

It may well be that the rise of China will facilitate this process, as China's authoritarian regime has little interest in democracy. Or it may be that responses to the COVID-19 pandemic will lead to the institutionalisation of more authoritarian powers in many countries, as governments round the world pass laws to give themselves increased emergency powers and roll out new surveillance technologies to monitor and control citizens' movements.

A   Chinese President Xi Jinping arrives at the 2019 G20 Summit, where he called for renewed efforts of global governance in order to ensure the continuation of unimpeded free trade.

B   Chinese President Xi Jinping (back right) and Kenyan President Uhuru Kenyatta (back left) attend a signing ceremony during the first Belt and Road Forum in Beijing, China, May 2017. The new forum is an attempt to create an alternative platform for international cooperation shaped by China rather than the US. Chinese state media dubbed it 'Globalization 2.0'.

However it happens, this scenario will lead to a dark vision of globalization, with authoritarian governments controlling their citizens and suppressing protest, while the wealthy elite accumulate more wealth in the unfettered global economy and inequality soars to new heights.

The **Belt and Road Initiative** is a multi-billion-dollar development strategy adopted by the Chinese government in 2013. Its main focus is developing rail and road infrastructure (belts) and maritime shipping routes (roads) to better connect Asia, Africa and Europe.

An **authoritarian** regime is a form of government characterized by strong central power that is maintained by political repression, the exclusion of opposition parties and the widespread limitation of civil liberties.

A

B

In the de-globalization scenario, we maintain national sovereignty and democracy, but we lose intense economic globalization.

Economic globalization would go into reverse and we would revert to a much looser degree of economic integration. States would take measures to limit the free flow of capital or goods across borders, and rates of international trade, foreign direct investment and capital market flows would decrease. The resulting moderate degree of economic integration, in which states would be free of the disciplinary power of global capital, would be accompanied by a thin layer of international rules, which leave plenty of policy space for national governments to decide on their own economic approaches and to be responsive to their citizens in a well-functioning national democracy.

A

Protectionist policies are those that seek to shield national producers, businesses and workers from foreign competitors. They typically include tariffs and quotas on imported goods.

A The terrorist attack on the twin towers of the World Trade Center, New York, 11 September 2001. At the time it was widely thought that this attack would lead to the end of globalization, but despite the subsequent 'war on terror', globalization continued apace.

B A 'Made in the USA' sign on a rack of clothing in California, USA, (above) and 'Buy British' signs on a farm in the UK (below) show a growing sense of economic nationalism in these countries as producers try to encourage consumers to buy local products.

B

Some observers argue that this is already beginning to happen, and there are indeed some indications that economic globalization has slowed down since the 2008 financial crisis and suggestions that it will decline still further in the wake of the COVID-19 pandemic.

In the past ten years, there has been a sharp drop in foreign direct investment and increasing restrictions imposed on cross-border trade and capital flows. A number of countries have implemented a range of protectionist measures. Most recently, under Trump, the USA has withdrawn from a number of major trade deals and started to try to bring production back within its borders. Data suggests that the number of TNCs that earn at least a quarter of their revenue abroad is beginning to decrease.

It is still too early to know whether this is a blip or a new trend, but there are many commentators, including Michael O'Sullivan, Stephen D. King, John Raulston Saul and Antimo Verde, who are already proclaiming that globalization is dead.

A

The de-globalization scenario could play out in different ways. One possibility is the 'nationalism' option, in which contemporary de-globalization could follow a similar path to the period of de-globalization that took place in the early 20th century, when the first period of globalization collapsed into economic nationalism and war.

Now, as then, the social costs of unregulated economic globalization are becoming too much, and we are witnessing the emergence of right-wing populist 'strong man' leaders who scapegoat foreigners and minorities and promise to make their nations great again. Scholars such as historian Niall Ferguson fear that a major war could well be on the horizon.

Another, more optimistic, possibility is what we might call 'democratic internationalism'. If states can be sufficiently freed from the disciplining power of global capital then they can implement policies that improve the lives of their citizens, thereby ending austerity, stimulating local economic development and reducing inequality.

The remaining thin layer of international rules should be reformed and democratized so that effective international action can be coordinated to rein in the power of global finance, organize a balanced rules-based system of trade and mobilize effective action on climate change, and other global problems. Over the years, non-governmental organizations (NGOs) and social movements have begun to shift away from campaigning against aspects of the global economic system and have started to advocate for alternatives. They have started to push for institutional reforms that would change the basic workings of the global economy.

Two of the most interesting institutional reform ideas that have emerged are the proposals for a currency transaction tax and a sovereign debt workout mechanism.

Non-governmental organizations are non-profit, citizen-based groups that function independently of government. Many play a major role in humanitarian response, international development and human rights. They have increased in number and importance since the 1980s and are considered a key feature of contemporary globalization.

A   The test firing of the Pukguksong-3, a new submarine-launched ballistic missile, off North Korea, October 2019.
B   NGOs are increasingly taking their concerns to the UN and seeking to become involved in global governance. Here an Oxfam representative speaks at the UN Security Council, January 2016 (above) and hundreds of NGOs participate in a UN civil society conference, August 2018 (below).

The idea of a currency transaction tax was first suggested by US economist James Tobin (1918–2002) in 1972. As the Bretton Woods system of monetary management fell apart and the world shifted to a system of floating exchange rates, Tobin foresaw that people would start to gamble, or speculate, on the rise and fall of currencies relative to other currencies and that this activity would have negative consequences for national economies and a destabilizing effect on the global economy.

He proposed the creation of a tax on currency transactions as a way to slow down the growth of this type of activity. He suggested that a small tax, of around 0.1 to 0.5%, would deter short-term speculative exchanges while having little effect on international trade. The idea, as he put it, was to 'throw sand in the wheels of currency speculation'. His idea lay dormant for 25 years until 1997, when Spanish journalist Ignacio Ramonet brought it back to life in an editorial for the French newspaper *Le Monde diplomatique*. In 1998, ATTAC (Association for a Tobin Tax in Aid of Citizens) was formed and started to campaign strongly for the tax.

A

The **Robin Hood tax** is named after the legendary English folk hero who stole from the rich to give to the poor, and thus became a powerful symbol of the fight for justice.

A   Activists from ATTAC dressed as influential world leaders squeeze a large inflated rubber globe in a protest against global 'belt-tightening' austerity measures, before the G20 Summit in Hamburg, Germany, July 2017.
B   An activist dressed as Robin Hood rolls a giant One Euro coin during a protest in Berlin, Germany, June 2011.
C   Campaigners for a Robin Hood Tax protest outside Barclays Annual General Meeting in London, UK, April 2012.

Many activists in the 'global justice movement' became interested in the tax and emphasized the huge amounts of revenue – estimated at around $300 billion per year – that it could generate. They renamed it the 'Robin Hood tax' and saw it as a way of carrying out taxation and redistribution at the global level, redistributing wealth from global elites who make money in the financial sector to poor people in the developing countries.

Since then, various types of currency transaction tax have been discussed and debated, and suggestions have also broadened out to include a more general tax on a wider variety of financial transactions. In recent years, several governments have implemented limited types of financial transaction tax in their own countries. However, while the idea of a global currency transaction tax has been discussed at the highest levels, for example by the G20, to date it is yet to be implemented and campaign work continues.

The idea of a sovereign debt workout mechanism first emerged in the 1990s, in the wake of the debt crisis experienced by most developing countries.

However, to this day, there is no systematic process under which sovereign debt restructurings take place and no bankruptcy code for countries to legally discharge unpayable debt. Instead, as discussed in previous chapters, debt restructuring is a highly political process and often comes with wide-ranging policy conditions imposed by creditors.

A

B

Bankruptcy is a legal process through which people or companies who cannot repay debts to creditors may seek relief from a court so that some or all of their debts are either restructured or wiped clean. Before the creation of bankruptcy law, it was common that a person who could not repay a debt would be forced into 'debt slavery', working for their creditor and repaying the debt with physical labour. Today, most countries have bankruptcy laws. However, there is no international system allowing a state to declare bankruptcy.

A   A masked Indonesian protester holds a banner during a 'drop the debt' demonstration in Jakarta, June 2005.

B   Protesters draped in the flags of developing countries call for the cancellation of third world debt during the G20 Finance Ministers meeting, Baden-Baden, Germany, March 2017.

C   A visualization of sovereign debt, 2018. The size of each country corresponds to its debt to GDP ratio. Countries with ratios over 50% are coloured red, those with ratios below 50% are green. Even though many developed countries have large debts, sovereign debt is a bigger problem for developing countries because their economies and credit ratings are weaker and they have to pay higher interest rates.

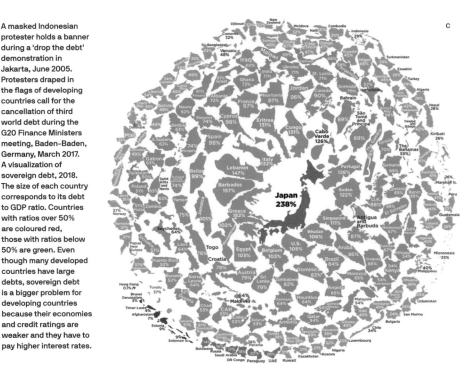

A large coalition of NGOs and social movements has, therefore, recently taken up the call for the creation of a sovereign debt arbitration tribunal. They argue that in order to de-politicize debt, and to help debt-ridden countries either reduce debt or restructure their payments in a more sustainable fashion, a new institution should be established to provide a comprehensive and impartial decision-making process, independent of both debtors and creditors, one that would be able to enforce its rulings. In the most serious cases, countries would be able to declare bankruptcy and have their debts completely wiped out, enabling them to turn over a new leaf and start again.

As a result of this campaigning work, an Ad Hoc Committee on Sovereign Debt Restructuring Processes was established at the UN in 2015 to look into the matter. However, the outright opposition of the developed countries, which have so far simply refused to take part in the process, has hampered its efforts. With sovereign debt levels rising rapidly due to the costs of tackling the COVID-19 pandemic, it is possible that there may be more political will to consider this in the coming few years.

A

Several academics, politicians and activists have sought to combine various reform proposals into a coherent package to bring about democratic internationalism at either the regional or the global level.

At the regional level, for example, a number of Latin American countries came together in 2004 to form ALBA (Bolivarian Alliance for the Americas) and tried to detach themselves from the global economy and to integrate in an alternative, more socially oriented manner. Building on the ideas of Keynes, they set up a regional clearing union and their own regional currency, the sucre. This enabled them to save foreign currency and reduce dependence on the US dollar, thus giving them more policy space to make their own economic decisions.

Perhaps the most developed set of ideas regarding democratic internationalism at the global level are those put forward by Heikki Patomäki and his colleagues. His proposal has four steps and a suggestion for transformative action to make it happen.

International law
is law that governs
the relations
between sovereign
states. However,
international
law is not legally
binding and there
is no enforcement
mechanism. If a
government wants
to make international
law binding in its own
country it has to write
the provisions into
its own domestic law.

**Democratization
of international
organizations** is
the process of
increasing their
democratic quality.
The World Bank
and IMF are highly
non-democratic
because voting rights
are apportioned
according to
financial contribution.
The rich countries
have the majority
of the votes and
thus control the
decision-making.

A   Latin American
leaders at the ALBA
Summit in Venezuela,
April 2007. ALBA seeks
a more progressive
form of integration,
different to the neoliberal
model of Mercosur or
the EU. Their initiatives
include forming 'grand
national companies'
as alternatives to TNCs,
and various transnational
health and welfare
programmes.

First, he argues that states must be at least partially freed from the disciplinary power of global capital so that they will have more autonomy to implement locally chosen, people-friendly policies. He believes that this can be best achieved by instituting a global currency transaction tax in order to slow down financial speculation, and by creating a sovereign debt workout mechanism so that debtor countries will not be bound by the policy demands of their creditors.

Second, the WTO would be reformed so that the world trade regime could be more socially oriented, rather than based on the logic of free trade.

Third, there needs to be a harmonization of international law. At present, international law is fragmented and incoherent. Sometimes international trade law says one thing while international human rights law says another, and it is not clear which law has precedence. This allows powerful individuals and corporations to find creative explanations for why their activities should be considered lawful. Patomäki suggests that a new democratic body should be created to determine which law applies in which situation and thus to bring order and coherence to the international legal system.

And fourth, there should be a process of democratization of international organizations, including the IMF, World Bank and others. Patomäki suggests that each organization would replace its existing (non-democratic) governance structure with a 'council of ministers', which would represent states, and a 'democratic assembly', with representatives of national parliaments and of civil society.

This proposed system would still be 'international', as no overarching body or powers would be created and states would retain their prerogative for law making and law enforcement. As it evolved and developed, what would emerge is a kind of non-centralized, non-territorial and non-exclusive system of complex democratic global governance.

How could these changes actually be brought about in practice? Patomäki suggests that activists from different countries should come together to form a global political party working towards this shared vision.

A global political party is a potential form of globalized political agency in pursuit of a broad programme of societal reorganization on a global scale. It would unite people from different countries in a shared political struggle beyond their national borders. Global parties could contribute to the formation of a global demos, a pluralist political community of world citizens exercising political rights in a globalized public sphere.

A

A European Spring is a transnational political party formed in 2019 to stand in the European Parliament elections. Representatives in different European countries support the same manifesto with the key aim to democratize the EU. Candidates promise that if elected to the European Parliament they will use their position to work towards the creation of a Pan-European Constitutional Assembly, whose members would then draft a democratic European Constitution.

B US Senator Bernie Sanders (above) and former Greek Finance Minister Yanis Varoufakis (below) recently joined forces to form the Progressive International, a kind of proto global political party launched in May 2020. The PI brings together movements, trade unions, political parties and academics to create a shared vision of a progressive world order and to design the policies needed to bring it to reality.

A **global political party** would
be a transnational political
association able to bring about
change on a global scale.
Political parties first emerged
in the 18th and 19th centuries,
alongside sovereign states
and national democracy.
As the world has globalized,
political parties have remained
at the national level, while
transnational activism has
increasingly been carried
out by networks of NGOs and
social movements. However,
their impact has been limited
because they have no shared
vision of global society, no
democratic legitimacy and
no political power. A global
political party would be a
stronger form of organization
to drive global political change.

B

Local chapters of this party could stand in national
elections, and, if successful, could then use their position
in state office to further the shared vision in existing
international institutions. They could take part in creating
new international law and steer it in a more socially oriented
direction, and they could also push for reforms of existing
international organizations. And, if this party were to come
into government in a number of powerful countries, it could
form a 'coalition of the willing', who would move forward
with creating new international organizations, such as
the tax body and the sovereign debt workout institution.

Democratic internationalism thus offers a positive vision of the de-globalization scenario, avoiding the threats of war and xenophobia that come with nationalism, and offering a road map to a potentially fairer and less tightly integrated world order.

In the final scenario, that of de-nationalism, we would retain globalization and democracy, but lose sovereign states. Politics would be scaled up to the global level to create a democratic federal world government.

The global government would regulate the global market and transnational corporations, maintain global financial stability and implement systems of global taxation and redistribution in accordance with the democratically expressed wishes of the whole of humanity. It would also implement global public health policies and coordinate swift and fair action in response to pandemics. And it could set global environmental policies, such as reducing carbon emissions, which would enable a truly global response to climate change.

Instead of a system of competing states, with each country trying to satisfy its own national interest irrespective of the fate of the world as a whole, this scenario would lead to world federation – a democratic 'United States of Earth'.

A

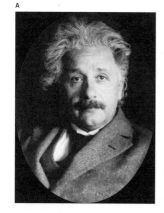

A Albert Einstein, Mahatma Gandhi, and Léopold Senghor all supported the idea of a democratic world federation. Senghor, the first president of Senegal, was also vice president of the early World Federalist Movement.

B President Barack Obama hands UN Secretary General Ban Ki Moon official documents for the US to join the Paris Climate Agreement, 2015. International treaties have limited effectiveness because states can leave when they wish. In 2019 President Donald Trump announced the US would leave the treaty.

B

This scenario, which can be termed 'democratic globalism', is the long-term vision favoured by scholars such as Luis Cabrera, Christopher Chase-Dunn and Raffaele Marchetti. They argue that in the current international system, states cannot stop corporations from disrupting ecological systems, legislate to reduce carbon emissions, or raise taxes to pay for public health, without fearing that corporations will simply relocate to another country.

Furthermore, in a system in which states have to compete with each other, they contend that there is no way to work together towards a common global good. Instead, states argue for their own national interests when negotiating international treaties and agreements, and in the resulting compromise international treaties are simply an inadequate and ineffective lowest common denominator. Thus, they insist that the international system and international law are fundamentally not fit for the purpose of dealing with shared global matters.

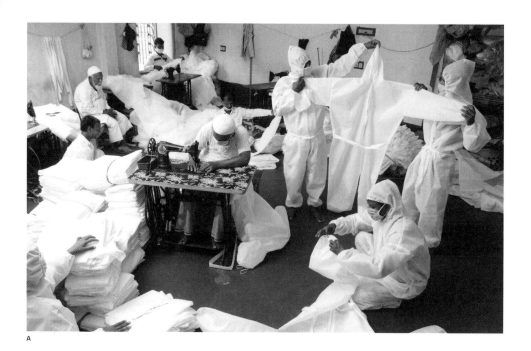

A

Many would claim that the failure of international cooperation during the COVID-19 pandemic shows clearly how the current international system does not work well. States have failed to share important health information, lack an agreed data reporting framework, and are competing against each other to buy ventilators, tests and personal protective equipment. This has resulted in delays in understanding the nature of the new disease, increased prices for crucial medical equipment, and a distribution of this equipment based on wealth rather than need. Because of these dynamics many developing countries have not been able to source the necessary tests and medical equipment, and face the likelihood of extremely high mortality rates. Not only is this deeply unjust, but in our highly interconnected world it ultimately places the rich countries in danger too, as the extremely contagious coronavirus which causes COVID-19 will surely quickly spread again around the world if it is left thriving in any one place. Infectious diseases do not respect borders and cannot be dealt with on a national basis.

Instead, they insist that a truly global system is necessary to be able to adequately deal with global problems, such as climate change, pandemics and economic stability and justice.

Supranational means 'beyond' or 'above' the national. In a supranational system, states pool some of their sovereignty into a political entity that exists beyond or above the individual states and that has power over those states. By contrast, in an international system, states retain full sovereignty and seek to negotiate various forms of (voluntary) cooperation.

Global law would be law that applies directly to everyone on the planet. In contrast to international law, it would be created by a democratically elected global legislature and enforced by a global police force and global courts with universal jurisdiction.

These scholars argue for the creation of a **supranational** system, with a democratic federal world government, a democratically elected world parliament that can legislate **global law**, and global courts that can interpret and enforce this law everywhere. The highest level of the federal global government would be able to effectively regulate transnational corporations and to make global policies which balance economic issues with those of health, environment and social well-being. The world parliament would be highly democratic, with a combination of elected representatives and active citizen participation so that decision-making could be truly democratized. Elites would not be able to opt out or create loopholes that make the whole system ineffective, and no person and no state would be above the law.

Citizens would vote at many different levels, from the local to the global. Major aspects of economic, public health and environmental policy would be set at the global level, while other matters would more likely be decided at local levels. Cultural diversity and local autonomy would be able to coexist alongside a small but important number of universal norms and laws.

A   Local production of personal protective equipment during the COVID-19 pandemic, Kolkata, India, April 2020. Competition between countries to procure vital equipment resulted in severe distribution problems and substantial price rises.

B   The European Union, symbolized here in this statue of the goddess Europa, is a supranational entity in which member states pool some of their sovereignty. It has a system of multi-level governance, in which citizens vote at both the national and European levels, and a form of supranational law which can be enforced by national or European courts.

B

A   Logo of the Global
Campaign to Dismantle
Corporate Power, a
transnational network
of some 250 social
movements, trade unions
and communities affected
by the activities of TNCs.
One of their demands
is for the creation of
binding international
law, enforced by a global
court, to compel TNCs
to respect human rights.
B   An investor rests in front
of trading screens in
Beijing, China, 2019.
The financial sector
would contract
significantly and the
economy would 'de-
financialize' if a universal
shared currency were
introduced.

A

In such a system, they argue, it would be possible
to truly implement universal human rights for
everyone and to back them up with the force
of law. States would not be able to hide behind
the mask of sovereignty and mistreat minorities
or other dissidents, because all citizens would
be able to take complaints to a global human
rights court. It would not be possible for TNCs
to commit human rights abuses in one place
and then avoid accountability on the basis
that its legal form exists only in another place.
Instead, TNCs would be treated as a unified
entity and they would be held to account
in the same global human rights court.

A democratic global tax body would reform the international
tax system into a global tax system, shutting down tax havens,
closing loopholes and taxing TNCs as singular entities on their
total global profits. If global citizens voted to do so, the global tax
body could also institute a range of global taxes in order to raise
revenue and carry out redistribution from the rich to the poor.
This would be the body that could institute the global wealth
tax, for example, that was recently suggested by Thomas Piketty,
in which a 1% tax could raise more than $1.5 trillion per year,
enough to bring everyone out of extreme poverty and to improve
the lives and livelihoods of people around the world. Revenues
could be used to fund health, education and welfare provision
for everyone, creating a kind of global welfare state.

Furthermore, the creation of a truly integrated global economy with one currency, one central bank, one monetary policy and one fiscal policy would eradicate the system of separate national economies and currencies in which financial speculators essentially gamble on the relative performance of one country against another.

Human rights are the rights, enshrined in the Universal Declaration of Human Rights (1948), that all human beings should have, whatever their nationality, age, ethnic origin, location, language, religion, ethnicity or any other status. However, because human rights are protected by international law, and not by a universal global law, they cannot be enforced.

Global taxes could include a carbon tax, with the aim of reducing carbon emissions and slowing down climate change; or a natural resources tax, with the aim of discouraging the extraction of non-renewable natural resources, such as oil, gas and minerals. Revenues from these taxes could be spent on developing clean energy and sustainable technologies.

Whereas a currency transaction tax in an international system would reduce such speculative activity, the creation of a single currency in a fully integrated global economy would simply bring this area of financial activity to an end, as there would be no separate currencies on which to gamble. In a similar way, there would be no separate economies with separate interest rates and thus speculators would no longer be able to gamble on relative changes in interest rates. Thus, a large proportion of the speculative financial activity that has damaged the real economy and led to increasing inequality would be brought to an end.

B

A After the experience of the Greek debt bailout showed that states could not implement the democratic wishes of their population against the powers of transnational finance, DiEM25 was set up as a new transnational movement with the aim of democratizing the EU and taming the banks. DiEM25 was instrumental in founding the European Spring party.

B Activists call for the creation of a World Parliament, Ventotene, Italy 2015.

Various ideas have been put forward regarding how to move towards this kind of democratic globalism. Cabrera has argued that the first step could be to form democratic integrated regional blocs, and that later these blocs would themselves integrate into one unified global entity. In this approach, regional integration initiatives, such as the EU, Mercosur and the African Union (AU), would be encouraged to integrate more deeply and to democratize until they take the form of a regional democratic federation. In the EU, currently the most integrated regional organization, there are several activist groups, including the European Federalist Movement and the Democracy in Europe Movement 2025 (DiEM25), that are campaigning for the EU to integrate further until it becomes a democratic federation.

Others instead suggest that it would be better to start working towards global integration right from the beginning. Many of these proposals envisage reforming the UN so that it could evolve into some kind of world government. A new assembly of directly elected citizen representatives would be added to form a kind of world parliament, which would be able to make world law, and the extensive UN bureaucracy would become a global civil service.

A

B

The **EU**, or European Union, was officially formed in 1992, having evolved out of the earlier European Coal and Steel Community. It has developed an internal single market in which there is free movement of people, goods, services and capital. It currently consists of 27 member states, who cover a total area of over 4 million km² and have a combined population of around 500 million, making it the largest combined economy in the world.

Mercosur is a Latin American trade bloc that was founded in 1991.

The **African Union (AU)** is a regional union consisting of 55 member states in Africa that was founded in 2001.

Perhaps the most developed initiative in this area is the Campaign for a United Nations Parliamentary Assembly, which advocates for the creation of a second UN chamber, alongside the General Assembly, to more directly represent the interests of world citizens.

In the short term, this would give parliamentarians from opposition parties a voice in international politics, and over time it could evolve into a properly democratic world parliament with directly elected citizen representatives and the ability to legislate world law.

A The International Criminal Court's chief prosecutor, Fatou Bensouda (centre), speaks at a press conference in Kinshasa, Democratic Republic of the Congo, May 2018.

B Youth activist Greta Thunberg berates world leaders for not taking action to deal with climate change at the UN Climate Action Summit, New York, USA, September 2019.

A

Another proposal focuses on increasing participatory democracy at the global level, by promoting the creation of a World Citizens' Initiative (WCI) at the UN. Modelled on the European Citizens' Initiative, the WCI would enable anyone in the world to raise an issue which, if supported by a certain number of world citizens, would then have to be formally discussed at one of the UN bodies, such as the General Assembly or the Security Council.

Participatory democracy is a form of democracy that emphasizes citizen involvement in political decision-making. New blockchain technologies could be used to enable much greater participation in a future global democracy.

An alternative approach suggests that the first supra-national bodies that should be created are global courts. Initially these courts could rule on international law and over time they would be the institutions that would be able to rule on emerging global law. The International Criminal Court (ICC) is an example of a supra-national court. It was founded in 2002 after a successful campaign by a large coalition of NGOs and social movements, and is the first quasi global court able to prosecute individuals, including heads of state, for the international crimes of genocide, crimes against humanity, war crimes and crimes of aggression.

B

Like the de-globalization scenario, the de-nationalism scenario also includes darker options. Some argue that a world government, even if democratically elected, could turn into a global tyranny. These are real concerns and any model of democratic globalism would need to make detailed proposals for how powers would be checked and balanced both vertically and horizontally and how democracy would be protected from the influences of money and power.

The options of democratic internationalism and democratic globalism would both appear to have great potential for reforming the world system and making globalization work, not only for the wealthy elite, but also for all of humanity.

Conclusion

A

Globalization as we know it is at a tipping point.

The establishment path appears to lead to globalization continuing in its current form, eroding democracy and becoming more authoritarian over time. The right-wing populist path promises de-globalization and nationalism. The transnational left-wing populists perhaps offer a route towards a more democratic form of globalization. Will globalization collapse or can it be transformed so that it can succeed?

History has shown that globalization has risen and fallen before. Many of the problems of contemporary globalization, including rising inequality, the concentration of power in huge transnational corporations and increasing tensions between elites and ordinary people, were also present in the first period of globalization in the 19th century. At the start of that period, states were not democratic and globalization could, therefore, proceed without having to take the concerns of workers and ordinary people into account. The establishment of democracy at the national level changed that and ultimately led to the breakdown of the system and the end of that period of globalization.

Will globalization fall again now? It is certainly a possibility.

A   Banksy street art in Chinatown, Boston, USA. With the growing social, economic and racial inequalities in today's world, many people are finding that their dreams are not within their reach.

B   Planes grounded at Heathrow airport during the COVID-19 lockdown. The aviation industry, one of the main vectors of global interconnectivity, came to an almost complete halt during the pandemic.

B

While democracy has been severely eroded in recent years, it is still functioning to some extent. And it has been through democratic elections that people have voted in right-wing populist leaders who promise de-globalization and nationalism. So, it is certainly possible that these leaders will implement policies to restrict international trade and international capital flows and try to bring economic activity back within their national borders.

A

A   Jeff Schoep, former chairman of the National Socialist Movement, speaks during a rally in Little Rock, Arkansas, USA, November 2018 (above). A man wears a jacket, saying 'Support your race' at a Neo Nazi Rally in Dortmund, Germany, May 2019 (below).

B   Soldiers of the Swiss army look at Android and iOS smartphones during a test of a new contact-tracing smart phone app being developed at the Swiss Federal Institute of Technology during the COVID-19 pandemic, April 2020. While this type of surveillance technology may be useful during the pandemic, there are fears about privacy, security and potential human rights abuses if governments try to continue its use after the emergency is over.

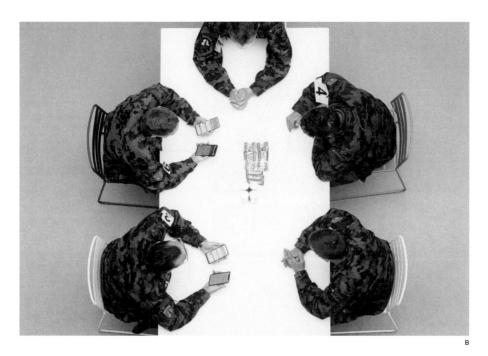

B

However, history has also shown that nationalism is not the answer. Xenophobia, racism and increasing competition between states has only led to conflict and war. The increasingly aggressive stance of the USA, the growth of anti-Islamic sentiment and the moves of several nationalist governments to limit the rights of ethnic minorities certainly do not bode well.

On the other hand, if globalization continues in its present form then the future also looks bleak, with the further dismantling of national democracy and the rise of totalitarian regimes that keep the masses in check while the middle classes fall into poverty and economic inequality rises to new proportions. Surely, this is not a globalization that anyone (except perhaps the elite) would want to succeed.

So, if neither globalization nor de-globalization can succeed, what is the answer?

A   A creative, non-violent protest-performance by Extinction Rebellion (XR) activists in Berlin, Germany, October 2019. XR is an international movement that uses civil disobedience to try to persuade governments to take urgent action on climate change, biodiversity loss and ecological collapse.

B   Umbrella artwork of the Occupy Central Love and Peace movement in Hong Kong, October 2014. The movement uses creative art and civil disobedience to push for democratic reforms in Hong Kong.

C   A banker walks past a protest tent in the financial district of London, UK, during the Occupy London protest of 2011.

It seems that the best option for humanity, perhaps the only option, is a radically transformed type of globalization that is more democratic and more responsive to the concerns of ordinary people.

In Chapter 4, we discussed a number of possible alternatives, under the broad headings of 'democratic internationalism' and 'democratic globalism'. These options offer hope for a more just and democratic form of globalization and seem to present the best chances for creating a type of globalization that can succeed – a type of globalization that gives everyone a voice and that unites humanity to be able to work together to solve shared global problems, such as climate change, pandemics and inequality.

Perhaps the shock of the COVID-19 pandemic, and the deep economic recession which is likely to follow it, will lead to a widespread realization that the current system is not working, and will open up a new window of opportunity for change.

Democracy has never been freely given; it has always had to be won. It is fundamentally about challenging the power of elites and spreading power more equally in society. When power is in the hands of elites, policies tend to promote their interests and often put wealth accumulation above all else. When power is distributed more equally, policies tend to address a wider range of societal concerns, and wealth accumulation is balanced against other issues such as health, pollution and climate change. It took massive political struggle throughout the 19th and early 20th centuries for democracy to be won at the state level, and only after it was in place did states respond to citizens' concerns regarding public health care, education and environmental regulation.

The effort to democratize globalization and bring about a truly global democracy, able to deal with the pressing global problems of our times, may be the most important struggle of the 21st century.

c

Further Reading

Archibugi, Daniele, *The Global Commonwealth of Citizens: Towards Cosmopolitan Democracy* (Princeton, NJ: Princeton University Press, 2008)

Bhagavan, Manu, *India and the Quest for One World: The Peacemakers* (London: Palgrave Macmillan, 2013)

Bummel, Andreas, *A Renewed World Organization for the 21st Century* (Berlin: Democracy Without Borders, 2018)

Burbank, Jane and Cooper, Frederick, *Empires in World History: Power and the Politics of Difference* (Princeton, NJ: Princeton University Press, 2010)

Büthe, Tim and Mattli, Walter, *The New Global Rulers: The Privatization of Regulation in the Global Economy* (Princeton, NJ; Oxford: Princeton University Press, 2011)

Cabrera, Luis (ed.), *Institutional Cosmopolitanism* (New York, NY: Oxford University Press, 2018)

Cabrera, Luis, *Political Theory of Global Justice: A Cosmopolitan Case for the World State* (London; New York, NY: Routledge, 2004)

Chase-Dunn, Christopher and Lerro, Bruce, *Social Change: Globalization from the Stone Age to the Present* (Boulder, CO: Paradigm, 2013)

Crouch, Colin, *The Globalization Backlash* (Cambridge; Medford, MA: Polity Press, 2018)

Crouch, Colin, *Post-Democracy* (Oxford: Polity, 2004)

Cusack, Asa K. (ed.), *Understanding ALBA: Progress, Problems, and Prospects of Alternative Regionalism in Latin America and the Caribbean* (London: Institute of Latin American Studies, 2018)

DiEM25, 'A Manifesto for Democratizing Europe', *Democracy in Europe Movement* (2016)

Dunn, John, *Setting the People Free: The Story of Democracy* (London: Atlantic Books, 2006)

Fukuyama, Francis, *The End of History and the Last Man* (New York, NY: Free Press, 1992)

Freeman, Dena, 'De-Democratization and Rising Inequality: The Underlying Cause of a Worrying Trend', *LSE International Inequalities Institute Working Paper*, 12 (2017)

Gautney, Heather, *Protest and Organization in the Alternative Globalization Era: NGOs, Social Movements and Political Parties* (New York, NY: Palgrave Macmillan, 2010)

Gill, Stephen, *Power and Resistance in the New World Order* (Basingstoke: Palgrave Macmillan, 2003)

Held, David, *Global Covenant: The Social Democratic Alternative to the Washington Consensus* (Oxford: Polity, 2004)

Held, David and McGrew, Anthony, *Globalization/Anti-Globalization: Beyond the Great Divide* (Cambridge: Polity, 2007)

Leinen, Jo and Bummel, Andreas, *A World Parliament: Governance and Democracy in the 21st Century*, trans. Ray Cunningham (Berlin: Democracy without Borders, 2018)

Marchetti, Raffaele, *Global Democracy: For and Against* (Abingdon; New York, NY: Routledge, 2008)

Mazower, Mark, *Governing the World: The History of an Idea, 1815 to the Present* (New York, NY: Penguin, 2012)

Moffitt, Benjamin, *The Global Rise of Populism: Performance, Political Style and Representation* (Stanford, CA: Stanford University Press, 2016)

Monbiot, George, *The Age of Consent: Manifesto for a New World Order* (London: Flamingo, 2003)

Muhr, Thomas (ed.), *Counter-Globalization and Socialism in* the 21st Century: The Bolivarian Alliance for the Peoples of Our America (Abingdon; New York, NY: Routledge, 2013)

O'Sullivan, Michael, The Levelling: What's Next After Globalization? (New York, NY: PublicAffairs, 2019)

Patomäki, Heikki, Democratizing Globalization: The Leverage of the Tobin Tax (London: Zed Books, 2001)

Patomäki, Heikki and Teivainen, Teivo, A Possible World: Democratic Transformation of Global Institutions (London: Zed Books, 2004)

Piketty, Thomas, Capital in the Twenty-First Century: The Dynamics of Inequality, Wealth and Growth, trans. Arthur Goldhammer (Cambridge, MA: Harvard University Press, 2014)

Pogge, Thomas, World Poverty and Human Rights: Cosmopolitan Responsibilities and Reforms (Cambridge: Polity, 2002)

Reinhard, Wolfgang, A Short History of Colonialism (Manchester: Manchester University Press, 2011)

Rodrik, Dani, The Globalization Paradox: Democracy and the Future of the World Economy (New York, NY: W. W. Norton & Co, 2011)

Roper, Louis and Van Ruymbeke, Bertrand (eds.), Constructing Early Modern Empires: Proprietary Ventures in the Atlantic World, 1500–1750 (Leiden: Brill, 2007)

Rosenboim, Or, The Emergence of Globalism: Visions of World Order in Britain and the United States, 1939–1950 (Princeton, NJ: Princeton University Press, 2017)

Santos, Boaventura de Sousa, The Rise of the Global Left: The World Social Forum and Beyond (London: Zed Books, 2006)

Sassen, Saskia, Losing Control: Sovereignty in an Age of Globalization (New York, NY; Chichester: Columbia University Press, 1996)

Saul, John Ralston, The Collapse of Globalism: And the Reinvention of the World (London: Atlantic Books, 2005)

Schwartz, Herman, States Versus Markets: The Emergence of a Global Economy, 3rd ed. (Basingstoke: Palgrave Macmillan, 2010)

Schwartzberg, Joseph, Transforming the United Nations System: Designs for a Workable World (Tokyo; New York, NY: United Nations University Press, 2013)

Sehm-Patomäki, Katarina and Ulvila, Marko (eds.),

Global Political Parties (London: Zed Books, 2007)

Singh, Kavaljit, The Globalization of Finance: A Citizen's Guide (London: Zed Books, 1999)

Slobodian, Quinn, Globalists: The End of Empire and the Birth of Neoliberalism (Cambridge, MA: Harvard University Press, 2018)

Starr, Amory, Global Revolt: A Guide to the Movements against Globalization (London: Zed Books, 2005)

Stiflitz, Joseph, Globalization and its Discontents (London: Penguin, 2002)

Verde, Antimo, Is Globalization Doomed? The Economic and Political Threats to the Future of Globalization (Basingstoke: Palgrave Macmillan, 2017)

Walton, John and Seddon, David (eds.), Free Markets and Food Riots: The Politics of Global Adjustment (Oxford: Blackwell, 1994)

Wilder, Gary, Freedom Time: Negritude, Decolonization and the Future of the World (Durham: Duke University Press, 2015)

Woods, Ngaire, The Globalizers: The IMF, the World Bank, and Their Borrowers (Ithaca, NY: Cornell University Press, 2014)

Picture Credits

Every effort has been made to locate and credit copyright holders of the material reproduced in this book. The author and publisher apologize for any omissions or errors, which can be corrected in future editions.

a = above, b = below,
c = centre, l = left, r = right

65b BRYAN R. SMITH/
AFP via Getty Images
66 Siegfried Grassegger/
imageBROKER/
Shutterstock
67 Michael Brochstein/SOPA
Images/LightRocket via
Getty Images
68 Equitable Growth
69 Issouf Sanogo/
AFP via Getty Images
70 Guy Smallman/
Getty Images
71 Chesnot/Getty Images
72 Jim Watson/
AFP via Getty Images
73 Hindustan Times via
Getty Images
74 UNCTAD www.unctad.org
75 Martin Bernetti/AFP via
Getty Images
76–7 © Chris Steele-Perkins/
Magnum Photos
78 Oli Scarff/
AFP via Getty Images
79 Brandon Dill/Getty
Images
80a Pat Roque/AP/
Shutterstock
80b Thony Belizaire/
AFP via Getty Images
81 Omar Torres/
AFP via Getty Images
82 Hector Mata/
AFP via Getty Images
83a François Ancellet/
Gamma-Rapho
via Getty Images
83b Rodrigo Buendia/
AFP via Getty Images
84 Reuters/Paulo Santos
85 Reuters/Paulo Santos
86l Alain Guilleux/
Alamy Stock Photo
86r Megapress/
Alamy Stock Photo
87 UPI/Alamy Stock Photo
88al Alberto Paredes/
Alamy Stock Photo
88ar Bloomberg
via Getty Images
88bl Meiner/ullstein bild
via Getty Images
88br Vanderlei Almeida/
AFP via Getty Images
89 Guy Bell/Alamy
Stock Photo

90 Valerie Baeriswyl/
AFP via Getty Images
91l Mustafa Yalcin/Anadolu
Agency/Getty Images
91r Mehdi Taamallah/
NurPhoto via
Getty Images
92 Lukas Schulze/
Getty Images
93 Money Sharma/
AFP via Getty Images
94 Reuters/Darren Staples
95a © 2016 M. E. J. Newman
95b © 2016 M. E. J. Newman
96a Juan Karita/AP/
Shutterstock
96b Luis Acosta/
AFP via Getty Images
97 David Ramos/
Getty Images
98 Dimitrios Sotiriou/Pacific
Press/LightRocket
via Getty Images
99a Bauzen/GC Images
99b Jim Watson/
AFP via Getty Images
100–1 Thomas Trutschel/
Photothek
via Getty Images
102 Kevin Frayer/Getty
Images
103 The Washington Post
via Getty Images
105a Pool/Getty Images
105b Etienne Oliveau/Pool/
Getty Images
106 Sipa/Shutterstock
107a Bloomberg
via Getty Images
107b Photofusion/Universal
Images Group
via Getty Images
108l Xinhua News Agency/
Shutterstock
108r Xinhua News Agency/
Shutterstock
109a Pacific Press/
LightRocket
via Getty Images
109b Stuart Ramson/AP/
Shutterstock
110 Focke Strangmann/EPA/
Shutterstock
111a John Macdougall/AFP
via Getty Images
111b Miguel Medina/
AFP/GettyImages

112a Mast Irham/EPA/
Shutterstock
112b Lino Mirgeler/DPA/
AFP via Getty Images
113 How Much
114 Juan Barreto/
AFP via Getty Images
116 European Spring
117a The Washington Post
via Getty Images
117b Aris Messinis/
AFP via Getty Images
118l Bettmann
via Getty Images
118c Elliott & Fry/
Getty Images
118r Michel Laurent/Gamma-
Rapho via Getty Images
119 Reuters/Jonathan Ernst
120 Debajyoti Chakraborty/
NurPhoto via Getty
Images
121 Photo by Leon Neal/
Getty Images
122 Global Campaign to
Dismantle Corporate
Power, www.
stopcorporateimpunity.
org
123 Wang Zhao/
AFP via Getty Images
124 Panayotis Tzamaros/
NurPhoto via Getty
Images
125 Oded Gilad
126 John Wessels/
AFP via Getty Images
127 Stephanie Keith/
Getty Images
128–9 Frederick Florin/
AFP via Getty Images
130 The Boston Globe
via Getty Images
131 Simon Dawson/
Bloomberg
via Getty Images
132a Sachelle Babbar/ZUMA
Wire/Shutterstock
132b Reuters/Jim Urquhart
133 Laurent Gillieron/
EPA-EFE/Shutterstock
134a Christophe Gateau/dpa/
AFP via Getty Images
134b South China Morning Post
via Getty Images
135 In Pictures Ltd./
Corbis via Getty Images

Index

References to illustrations are in **bold**.

Acknowledgments:
I would like to thank all the team at Thames & Hudson, particularly Jane Laing, Tristan de Lancey, Phoebe Lindsley and Isabel Jessop, who pulled off the amazing feat of getting this book to production in the midst of lockdown conditions during the COVID-19 pandemic.

Special thanks also go to Yael Grant, Corinne Lang and Caroline Treitel for their encouragement and feedback, and to colleagues at the London School of Economics and Political Science for their intellectual fellowship and exchange.

This book is dedicated to Oded, who first inspired me to think globally.

MIX
Paper from responsible sources
FSC
www.fsc.org
FSC® C112556

First published in the United Kingdom in 2020 by Thames & Hudson Ltd, 181A High Holborn, London WC1V 7QX

First published in the United States of America in 2020 by Thames & Hudson Inc., 500 Fifth Avenue, New York, New York 10110

Can Globalization Succeed? © 2020
Thames & Hudson Ltd, London

Text © 2020 Dena Freeman
General Editor: Matthew Taylor

For image copyright information, see pp. 138–139

All Rights Reserved. No part of this publication may be reproduced or transmitted in any form or by any means, electronic or mechanical, including photocopy, recording or any other information storage and retrieval system, without prior permission in writing from the publisher.

British Library Cataloguing-in-Publication Data
A catalogue record for this book is available from the British Library

Library of Congress Control Number 2020931752

ISBN 978-0-500-29567-0

Printed and bound in Slovenia by DZS Grafik

Be the first to know about our new releases, exclusive content and author events by visiting
thamesandhudson.com
thamesandhudsonusa.com
thamesandhudson.com.au